Y0-CFS-086

Human Rights and Psychological Research

A DEBATE ON PSYCHOLOGY AND ETHICS

Based on the Loyola Symposium
on Psychology and Ethics, May 2, 1973

Edited by Eugene C. Kennedy

LOYOLA UNIVERSITY OF CHICAGO

Thomas Y. Crowell Company

New York   Established 1834

Copyright © 1975 by Thomas Y. Crowell Company, Inc.

All Rights Reserved

Except for use in a review, the reproduction or utilization of this work in any form or by any electronic, mechanical, or other means, now known or hereafter invented, including photocopying and recording, and in any information storage and retrieval system is forbidden without the written permission of the publisher. Published simultaneously in Canada by Fitzhenry & Whiteside, Ltd., Toronto.

Library of Congress Cataloging in Publication Data
Main entry under title:

Human rights and psychological research.

    Includes bibliographies and index.
    1. Human experimentation in psychology—Congresses. 2. Bioethics—Congresses. I. Kennedy, Eugene C., ed. II. Loyola Symposium on Ethics and Psychology, Chicago, 1973.
BF76.5.H85   174'.9'15   75-1206
ISBN 0-690-00804-X

Thomas Y. Crowell Company
666 Fifth Avenue
New York, New York 10019

Manufactured in the United States of America

Contents

Editor's Preface   vii
Eugene C. Kennedy

Foreword   xi
Kenneth Little

Chapter 1. Psychology and Ethics   1
M. Brewster Smith

Chapter 2. The Insights of the Judaeo-Christian Tradition and the Development of an Ethical Code   23
Richard A. McCormick, S.J.

Chapter 3. Metaethical and Normative Considerations Covering the Treatment of Human Subjects in the Behavioral Sciences   37
Diana Baumrind

Chapter 4. Ethical Issues in Research Involving Human Subjects   69
Ernest Wallwork

Chapter 5. It Neither Is Nor Ought To Be: A Reply to Wallwork   83
Diana Baumrind

Chapter 6. In Defense of Substantive Rights: A Reply to Baumrind   103
Ernest Wallwork

Appendix. Excerpts from "Ethical Principles in the Conduct of Research with Human Participants"   126
American Psychological Association

Index   143

Editor's Preface

The ethical questions that confront research psychologists are not theirs alone. America has become painfully and suddenly aware of a national sense of morality left too long unattended; Watergate has indeed been a watershed event in the shadow of which almost every profession has at least begun to reexamine the nature and operational efficacy of its ethical commitments. We seem, as a people, to be waking from a long dream in which our self-confident moral certainty almost guaranteed that our political, military, and educational undertakings were not only optimistically democratic but morally noble as well. That kind of righteousness proved to be a dangerous luxury because it muffled ethical inquiry in the name of working out the special American destiny of progress.

Nobody plans it that way, of course; it just gets to be that way when in church or state or scientific laboratory motivation and means are taken for granted. It is difficult for persons caught up in the middle of professional activity that seems to have been accepted by worthy colleagues for a long time to get enough distance to see themselves in practical ethical perspective. Perhaps we could discover ourselves in the middle of a moral maze built not only by us but by the general culture in which pragmatism has been such a powerful molding influence. Only here could a Saul Alinsky, confronting the conditions that demanded radical social responses, make the famous statement, "If the end doesn't justify the means, then what the hell does?" If we are confident of doing good, then we can proceed with untroubled consciences to do it. We are disturbed by questions that make us pause or have a momentary doubt about our resolve. After all, we are eradicating disease, fighting communism, discovering the secrets of our social interactions. What, then, could George Foster mean by his famous questions over a decade ago: "How far should we go in trying to help others?" and "What are our obligations, and what are the limits to these obligations?" (*Traditional Cultures and the Impact of Technology.* New York: Harper & Row, 1962.) Now, however, with a web of compromised ethical attitudes weighing down the spirit of the country, people are wondering how we journeyed so far without noticing what was happening to us. Former presidential aide Jeb Stuart Magruder spoke a phrase that many could understand when, facing prison, he reflected on how, caught up in the great events of the times, he had lost, almost carelessly, his "moral compass."

Science of all kinds became self-justifying in America, the scene of so many of its marvelous accomplishments. It came, in fact, to fuse its perception of its ends so that they were almost indistinguishable. New knowledge justified traditionally apolitical scientific endeavor, but the practical use of this knowledge, buoyed by economic incentives, was closely identified with the primary goal so that marketable developments were seldom subject to exhaustive ethical inquiry. The scientific community awoke one day to discover that it had given the world a nuclear suicide weapon; the second guesses about the morality of this achievement have never been persuasive enough to slow down the invention of more exquisite ordnance. Nor have the social sciences been immune from soul searching about the methods or implications of their research which has sometimes been used for ambiguous moral purposes. It all seemed integrated with national goals and security; one might notice how the supposed "scientific neutrality" of a field like psychology collapsed as it was gradually politicized. Thus Donald MacArthur of the Defense Department could, in an invited address to the American Psychological Association (APA) a few years ago, be quite clear about the way research would be funded:

> We make no apology for our insistence on relevance and on coupling of research activities to our basic continuing missions. We want to support the finest talent in the country in research important both to the growth of science and to the solution of national security problems. [Current

Editor's Preface

emphasis on the Department of Defense's social and behavioral sciences program, *Amercian Psychologist*, 1968, 23(2), 104–107.]

It is easy to be moralistic but extremely difficult to be moral. America, reeling from facing itself and the tangle of killing deception that was Vietnam, staggered within a few months into the morass of political falsehood that is Watergate. Theories of collective guilt are generally rhetorical and hard to sustain, and yet it would be difficult to say that any profession was completely free from contributing to or helping to sustain the illusion of assured moral force that guided us into such disasters. It was easy to make a case for the involvement of lawyers, clergymen, physicians, and psychologists—for all of us in one way or another—in letting too many hard questions about what we are doing or what we were ready to settle for slip by us unanswered. It is more important, however, to ask now where we stand and whether we are prepared to make the systematic inquiries into our professional activities to clarify their ethical foundation and purpose. We are only self-indulgently masochistic when we beat our breasts about what we may have failed to do; we are, by the very action, moral when we search now for the ethical substratum of our professional goals and methods.

A crystallizing moral awareness among scientists focuses not just on the purposes of research funders but on the aims and methods of researchers themselves. What came to be taken for granted as moral because of the overall good intentions of science is now sharply questioned. Earlier failure to take more account of the rights of research subjects may, in fact, have contributed to the growing national mistrust of professional researchers from all disciplines. Good ethics have, in fact, become a matter of enlightened self-interest for researchers.

It is not a task that is as yet wholeheartedly accepted by some professionals, even within the social sciences. Humphreys, for example, says that "there are no 'good' or 'bad' methods—only 'better' or 'worse' ones," and that "concern about 'professional integrity'... is symptomatic of a dying discipline. Let the clergy worry about keeping their cassocks clean; the scientist has too great a responsibility for such compulsions!" (L. Humphreys, *Tearoom Trade*. Chicago: Aldine 1970.) It is quite easy, as Harris Chaiklin has noted, for a researcher to make his investigative journey along "the borderline between naive intent and knowingly doing wrong." [*Current issues in mental health,* National Institute of Mental Health, publication no. (HSM) 73-9029, 1973, p. 40.] It is not easy to raise the pertinent questions about research procedures with human subjects, an area of explicit concern for psychologists and other social scientists even if there were no question of the way findings would be used by others.

Deception has been taken for granted, almost like graft in municipal government, for so long that it has seemed an accepted and acceptable part of the investigator's armamentarium. That psychology has persisted in asking hard questions about its own methods is to its credit. Appropriate parts of the guidelines for ethical research conduct, the fruit of a hard-working task force of the American Psychological Association, are printed in this book to attest to its continuing ethical awareness. The journey, however, is far from completed; it can only be finished when all practicing psychologists, in the context of their time, place, and activities, wrestle with the problems that are involved. It is precisely this which has not yet taken place, despite our national, personal, and professional conflicts, on a deep or pervasive level. Psychologists, like other men and women, have had other, seemingly more dominating interests. Indeed, some of these, such as involvement in advocacy groups fighting to have psychologists recognized by prospective national health legislation, have been almost all consuming. The technical discussion of ethical questions, when survival seems to be the issue, finishes last on the agenda of many busy professionals.

This volume provides focus on the ethical questions connected with human research that are most apposite for social scientists at the present time. Not only do the participants state the questions clearly but they also offer their own special perspectives on the pertinent issues. Beyond this, in the continuing exchange between Drs. Baumrind and Wallwork, we have a model for the kind of dialogue that can be carried out by researchers in a time of heightened ethical awareness. These are inquiries that cannot be postponed except at an extraordinarily high cost both to individual psychologists and to the profession of scientific and professional psychology.

Eugene C. Kennedy
LOYOLA UNIVERSITY OF CHICAGO

Foreword

In this symposium you will have many surprises. You will, for example, hear a theologian speak like a psychologist; a psychologist speak like a moral philosopher; and another psychologist who speaks, admittedly, as an ethicist and, by behavior, as a logician; and finally, a vice-chancellor who speaks as a scholar.

Father McCormick presents what I consider a fascinating paper, possibly because I did not expect a theologian to talk like a psychologist. He presents the thesis that professional codes in general are the end of a process occurring when the discipline feels that it must codify its behavior and its rules and regulations. I would agree with that, but I would emphasize that the process is an ongoing one; it is never a terminal one. The code that exists today exists to some extent for the environment in which it is made. Then, like a good psychologist, Father McCormick proceeds to identify the basic motives and drives—tendencies he calls them (you can call them genetic predispositions or what you will)—that represent the continuing urges of human beings. They constitute the nature of human nature. I would agree with the list, a partial one, that he gives, with slight variations. He writes about the tendency to exploratory behavior—and you can put a slash mark and say "curiosity" after that—which is probably the primary drive of the scientist. He also mentions the tendency to friendship, to which I would add "trust" as a component. As for the tendency toward skills and abilities, psychologists would probably say "development of skills and abilities/self-actualization." Similar modifications can be made to the rest of his list.

Most of these would probably be accepted by psychologists as prevailing tendencies in human beings. Some psychologists would hold out for autonomous drives, those that develop as a result of experience and which have the same primacy, at adulthood anyway, as those that perhaps have a more genetic basis. I agree, however, with McCormick's statement that these drives, tendencies, urges, motives—what have you—constitute the basis of our values and would also agree with his judgment that satisfaction of these drives should never be placed in opposition to one another. This is the point that Dr. Baumrind makes in insisting that research should be so designed that the researcher—the scientist—is not placed in a moral dilemma. Otherwise at that point he is going to have to put in conflict certain of these tendencies.

Dr. Baumrind's emphasis on rule-utilitarianism is very appealing to me because I am basically a law-and-order man. I think that laws are designed to increase our freedom and when you have violations of laws, you find that it results in a decrease in freedom. Unfortunately, there are laws *and* laws. Thus the general statement should probably be modified to say that good laws are designed to increase our freedom but there are also other laws. The Volstead Act was one which was repealed because it was considered to simply be restricting freedom and not increasing it.

I have several reservations to Dr. Baumrind's thesis, not on the basis of the type of impeccable logic presented by Dr. Wallwork, but because I think it implies an essential distrust of her fellow psychologists. She is asking, as is Dr. Wallwork, for commandments, for some "Thou shalt nots." These I find psychologically unsatisfactory. They require a degree of structure in the world that does not exist. Three thousands years after their issuance we still find people killing, stealing, lying, and coveting each other's spouses *regardless* of the Ten Commandments. They seem to go against the basic tendencies otherwise the violations would not occur; they must be antitendency.

Dr. Smith discusses the "political nature" of the development of the APA "Ethical Principles in the Conduct of Research with Human Participants." I think political nature is a good description of it; it is an intermediate step, not a terminal one. It is, in fact, an *intermediate point* in a process. I consider this code of ethics as simply one stage in the process of *persuading* psychologists to behave more ethically, rather than as an end in itself. Socialization, in the sense of the term

Foreword xiii

as Father McCormick uses it, comes about slowly, and I think it will require a fair amount of time before we will all look around at our fellow citizens and say they are behaving in a way that we consider ethical and responsible. If you have an ultimate goal in mind, you proceed by chaining responses, and the present APA code of ethics is one link in that chain. There will be a constant pressure on the psychologist/scientist even though the code has its loopholes. One might say that as a set of *commandments* the code is not satisfactory, but as a push in a given direction it is one stage in the process. The fact that it was arrived at in a democratic process, as a consensual thing, satisfying no one but acceptable to most, is perhaps what Father McCormick has in mind when he says that the development of codes must involve a wider group of individuals than those who were actually ultimately responsible for the code. In this case the wider group was confined to a single profession, that of psychology.

As an aside, Dr. Wallwork suggests that the *American Psychologist* establish a panel to determine whether the ethical research codes are observed in a conduct of studies reported in that journal. As editor of the *American Psychologist,* I work hard to keep experimental articles out of it, so his suggestion is not appropriate for that journal. It would apply to the other 13 journals that are substantively scientific in nature. APA's Publications and Communication Board, particularly the Council of Editors which reports to it, has been debating this question.

As I understand them, both Dr. Baumrind and Dr. Wallwork are using the term "cost-effective" in a highly limited sense; even industry and government, which originally developed the term, no longer use it in such a restricted sense. Part of the cost of any activity or function of an organization is psychic cost, the psychological expense to the individuals to whom this function will be applied. In a rational approach these are weighed—sometimes they are weighed in ways that are manipulative and deceitful—but at least they are taken into consideration. As an example of the manipulation, a few years back there was a strike of check-out clerks in a large grocery chain in one of the major cities of the country. The stores fought the strike for three days during which time the stores were closed down. Then they capitulated and gave the employees everything demanded. The decision to fight the strike and to resist the demands was not based on the demands themselves but on a cost-effectiveness analysis. The stores allowed the strike to occur and then yielded because this increased the morale of the employees tremendously. The amount of turnover in checkers was reduced dramatically and, since it cost the store $225 to train each checker, the stores came out ahead financially in the end. The grocery chain was able to reduce expenses and the employees got an increase in morale.

Dr. Smith does get into the issue of the application of ethical codes in the service area; most of these discussions are of *professional* codes of ethics. In this respect allow me to refer to a social perspective on professionalism which defines professional behavior in terms of four essential attributes: (1) a high degree of generalized and systematic knowledge; (2) a primary orientation toward the interests of the community, rather than to individual self-interest; (3) a high degree of individual self-control of behavior through codes of ethics; and (4) the internalization of these ethical codes in the process of work socialization.

The symposium members have discussed codes of ethics in terms of professional ethics; this always implies a power relationship. Such codes are sets of rules that will control one's behavior in having power over someone else: the therapist over the patient, the researcher over the subject, the teacher over the student, the tester over the testee. It is a method of control of the power of the individual in the superordinate position. Perhaps more needs to be said about what might be called the "upstream relationship." What about the relationship—the *ethics* of the relationship—of the subject to the experimenter? This was raised in the discussions of the APA code for research with human subjects. What obligation does the subject—or participant to avoid that term "subject"—have to the experimenter? What obligation or code of ethics rules the relationship of the student to the teacher? This question comes up at various times during student disruptions but probably not in terms of *ethics* since we rarely think of ethics as applying in this upstream fashion. We use other terms such as "responsibility" and "obligation." But I feel that it is probably as important an area to discuss as any other if we are going to talk about freedom, informed consent, and contracts arrived at freely. Contracts have two sides rather than one and the obligations go both ways. This issue needs considerably more discussion, even though in the usual professional code of ethics it always has a one-way direction.

Foreword

A responsible individual is one who has the capacity for moral and rational decisions, one who can be held accountable for his actions, and one who has a choice of a number of significant modes of behavior. Perhaps something similar to that can be worked into "an upstream code of ethics." In lieu of that, and with our admittedly fallible code of ethics for research with human subjects, I think that since I have sufficient trust in my fellow psychological scientists, I would simply ask that he or she act with informed *self-consent*— that they be informed by their peers or by surrogate groups and, in their consenting to do what they do as research workers, that they fully accept this responsibility.

Kenneth Little

AMERICAN PSYCHOLOGICAL ASSOCIATION

CHAPTER 1

Psychology and Ethics

M. Brewster Smith
University of California
Santa Cruz

For a psychologist who is not vested with the theological or the pastoral or the philosophical mantle to venture to talk to others about matters of ethics—rather than tending to the ethical problems in his own sphere of action—would seem to require some mixture of hubris and *chutzpah*. Since my claims as an ethical commentator are modest, I must set the context for my remarks so that my qualifications as a citizen-psychologist stand in for my obvious lack of special competence as a student of ethics.

Perhaps I can best serve this purpose and at the same time expose my stance on ethical issues if I begin with some brief comments on Diana Baumrind's excellent paper in the symposium for which this essay was written.[1] Since I put in several years of hard intermittent work as a member of Stuart Cook's Committee on Ethical Standards in Psychological Research that produced, after numerous revisions, the American Psychological Association document that Dr. Baumrind has subjected to such searching criticism, it is only fair to mention that, *unless* I were allowed to say a few words about her paper, I should find it hard to get on with the essay. Throughout the work of our committee, Dr. Baumrind was our most articulate critic. Her paper for this symposium develops her critical perspective in full explicitness, and I regard it as a substantial contribution to our shared objectives of raising the level of ethical sensitivity among psychologists and of improving the ethical level of common practice in psychological and other social behavioral research with human participants.

Quite properly, Dr. Baumrind set herself a task different from that of the committee. As a concerned, ethical individual, she has worked out her own coherent ethical perspective, developed in her paper in explicit relationship to the well-explored alternatives of ethical philosophy. She has applied that perspective to current practice in psychological research and to the Cook committee document, letting the chips fall where they may. For an individual critic, this is the strategy of choice—the way most likely to affect our actual ethical standards and behavior. Since I find both Dr. Baumrind's premises and conclusions attractive (though she is surer of her grounds than I can be of mine) I wish her well; I hope that as a result of her educational efforts, the next version of the APA code and commentary moves in the direction of her recommendations.

The committee's appropriate task could not be the one that Dr. Baumrind assigned to herself. In the human world in which we live, ethical issues are indissolubly commingled with political and educational ones, at least whenever the stakes are socially important. Divergent interests and value perspectives compete with one another

---

[1] The symposium focused especially on the code of "Ethical Principles in the Conduct of Research with Human Participants" adopted by the American Psychological Association (reproduced later in this paper). In the symposium Diana Baumrind gave a searching critique of the code and its approach to ethical problems, objecting to the pragmatic compromises embodied in it. The initial part of this essay is addressed to her criticism, but is intelligible without the context of her remarks.

politically; and efforts to raise one another's sensitivity to ethical considerations, to promote ethical awareness and ethical action as we ourselves best understand it, are inherently educational. A heterogeneous committee responsible to the membership of the American Psychological Association necessarily encountered ethical issues in a political and educational context unlike that of a single concerned individual. Even if we on the committee had been able to agree among ourselves on ethical first premises (although we educated one another and moved a considerable distance toward a consensual perspective, we could not claim *that*), we could not have imposed any single-minded view on the congeries of experimentalists and humanists and others who constitute American psychology—Festingerians; Skinnerians; Rogerians; students of test scores and stress, creativity, conformity, cognitive coding, and conservation—virtually all of them persons of goodwill who regard their different versions of the psychological enterprise as ethically legitimate.

The initial tack we took was empirical. We assembled, studied, and classified an enormous number of actual concrete instances of ethical issues, conflicts, and decisions in psychological research with human beings, collected in successive waves from questionnaires sent to fully two-thirds of the APA membership list. We also interviewed a large number of psychologists who occupied special positions that were likely to entail an informed and considered perspective on ethical issues in psychological research: for instance, department chairmen, journal editors, members of review panels, and writers on research ethics—including Dr. Baumrind. We eventually broadened our sights to include nonpsychologists whose perspectives we expected to be relevant to our task—especially in sociology and philosophy. All of this was in the attempt to assure that we addressed ourselves to real issues and that the perspectives which we brought to bear on the issues engaged and reflected the ethical thinking of the discipline, not just our personal principles or consciences.

From this foundation, we attempted to codify the principles that were involved in ethical decisions in the array of incidents before us. This was not an armchair job; it involved long and heated debates and reconsideration. Eventually we came forth with a draft version of principles and illustrative incidents that we published for reaction by the entire APA membership and sent to a large number of individuals, organizations, and local groups with a special invitation for comment. The reaction was explosive: it almost convinced us that our task was impossible. We were attacked from both flanks. (The comments often were accompanied by a few polite words recognizing our good intentions and hard work, and commiserating with our obvious failure.) On the one hand were those like Dr. Baumrind, who saw our product as a charter for Machiavellianism, an excuse for unethical practice. On the other were just as many who were sure that our proposed code would put scientific psychology out of business and who regarded the very publication of the draft document with its included incidents as an unmitigated disaster, perhaps even an unethical act. There were still others who found our long document with its detailed—I was about to say Jesuitical—analysis simply unreadable.

Chastened, we went back to the drawing board for a thoroughgoing revision—this time better informed about the political and educational problems that were enmeshed with the ethical ones, and impressed by the *lack* of ethical consensus among honorable persons in our discipline. We became more explicit in our realization that we could not be lawgivers, only sensitizers. We succeeded in compressing the many subprinciples of our first draft into a decalogue of 10 principles that phrased important ethical ideals. But, perforce, we eschewed the role of Moses. With important exceptions, we avoided the categorical "Thou shalt not . . . ," substituting, in effect, the more cautious "Thou shalt worry deeply, consult with others sincerely, and be prepared to justify thy decision to thy peers and the public if . . ." —if considerations of scientific gain seem to justify a limited compromise of ethical ideals. The Talmud or commentary that accompanied our decalogue discussed in detail the same ethical issues with which we had dealt in our previous, unacceptable document, taking into account the reactions that our earlier version received. Perhaps because the earlier version had aroused such anxiety and animosity, our revision proved widely acceptable when distributed for reaction to the entire membership. With only minor changes it was adopted in December 1972 as an official document of the American Psychological Association (Ad Hoc Committee, 1973). (The full title is "Ethical Principles in the Conduct of Research with Human Participants.")

> The decision to undertake research should rest upon a considered judgment by the individual psychologist about how best to contribute to psychological science and to human welfare. The responsible psychologist

Psychology and Ethics

weighs alternative directions in which personal energies and resources might be invested. Having made the decision to conduct research, psychologists must carry out their investigations with respect for the people who participate and with concern for their dignity and welfare. The Principles that follow make explicit the investigator's ethical responsibilities toward participants over the course of research, from the initial decision to pursue a study to the steps necessary to protect the confidentiality of research data. These Principals should be interpreted in terms of the context provided in the complete document offered as a supplement to these Principles.

1. In planning a study the investigator has the personal responsibility to make a careful evaluation of its ethical acceptability, taking into account these Principles for research with human beings. To the extent that this appraisal, weighing scientific and humane values, suggests a deviation from any Principle, the investigator incurs an increasingly serious obligation to seek ethical advice and to observe more stringent safeguards to protect the rights of the human research participant.

2. Responsibility for the establishment and maintenance of acceptable ethical practice in research always remains with the individual investigator. The investigator is also responsible for the ethical treatment of research participants by collaboration, assistants, students, and employees, all of whom, however, incur parallel obligations.

3. Ethical practice requires the investigator to inform the participant of all features of the research that reasonably might be expected to influence willingness to participate and to explain all other aspects of the research about which the participant inquires. Failure to make full disclosure gives added emphasis to the investigator's responsibility to protect the welfare and dignity of the research participant.

4. Openness and honesty are essential characteristics of the relationship between investigator and research participant. When the methodological requirements of a study necessitate concealment or deception, the investigator is required to ensure the participant's understanding of the reasons for this action and to restore the quality of the relationship with the investigator.

5. Ethical research practice requires the investigator to respect the individual's freedom to decline to participate in research or to discontinue participation at any time. The obligation to protect this freedom requires special vigilance when the investigator is in a position of power over the participant. The decision to limit this freedom increases the investigator's responsibility to protect the participant's dignity and welfare.

6. Ethically acceptable research begins with the establishment of a clear and fair agreement between the investigator and the research participant that clarifies the responsibilities of each. The investigator has the obligation to honor all promises and commitments included in that agreement.

7. The ethical investigator protects participants from physical and mental discomfort, harm, and danger. If the risk of such consequences exists, the investigator is required to inform the participant of that fact, secure consent before proceeding, and take all possible measures to minimize distress. A research procedure may not be used if it is likely to cause serious and lasting harm to participants.

8. After the data are collected, ethical practice requires the investigator to provide the participant with a full clarification of the nature of the study and to remove any misconceptions that may have arisen. Where scientific or humane values justify delaying or withholding information, the investigator acquires a special responsibility to assure that there are no damaging consequences for the participant.

9. Where research procedures may result in undesirable consequences for the participant, the investigator has the responsibility to detect and remove or correct these consequences, including, where relevant, longterm aftereffects.

10. Information obtained about the research participants during the course of an investigation is confidential. When the possibility exists that others may obtain access to such information, ethical research practice requires that this possibility, together with the plans for protecting confidentiality, be explained to the participants as part of the procedure for obtaining informed consent.

If a camel is a horse designed by a committee, one can hardly expect such a document to be purely equine, given the process by which it was conceived, gestated, and brought to delivery. It is a piece and a product of political and educational process in the realm of practical ethics, not an instantiation of abstract ethical philosophy. I believe that the wide participation of psychologists in its production has been an important venture in ethical education and that the document itself will prove helpful. But its principles and commentary do not solve the ethical problems of psychological research with human subjects; rather, they *display* these problems and put the responsibility for complex ethical decisions where it belongs, on the individual psychologist (who is obliged, of course, to take steps to counterbalance inevitable personal bias).

As in the venture of the Cook committee, I am concerned in the remainder of this essay with practical ethics for psychology and psychologists—ethics that are inextricably entangled with politics and education. I do not write from a technical philosophical position. The fact that in one of my roles I am an administrator as well as a psychologist leads me perforce to give substantial weight to the reality of conflict and to the necessity for compromise and accommodation if desirable human ends are to be realized. I readily grant Baumrind's point that an ethics of consensus can hardly be adequate philosophically, but I would stress, all the same, that the ethical consensus that *does* exist within a discipline or its components makes a big difference in how members of the discipline behave. Therefore I think it important to push consensus in the direction of humane values.

I share with Dr. Baumrind (but not with Skinner, 1971) a view of man as an actor, who at his best and in favorable situations is capable to an important degree—a crucial degree—of making responsible decisions. Such a view seems to be required if talk about ethics is to make any sense at all. I have stated this basic assumption carefully, recognizing that responsible decision is a difficult attainment, not a gift to be taken for granted. I also recognize that many positivistically inclined psychologists who do not conceive of man as a moral actor are nevertheless ethical in their own actions and favor good ethical practice. I only assert that the preconceptions of these positivists ill accord with the terms of ethical discourse.

I also share with Dr. Baumrind (but in this case not with Maslow, 1971, and similarly inclined humanistic psychologists) a sense of the reality of evil, which in my nontheological sense means that human beings cannot be assumed *naturally* disposed to always know their own good and to act in terms of it, and that in following their own natural impulses they can quite readily do harm to one another. We do not live in the Garden of Eden that some humanistic psychologists, and many of the romantic young, would like to wish into reality. (Here I find common ground with another humanistic psychologist —May 1972.) Our biological programming by no means guarantees that if the plant of human potential is watered properly, good will come of it. So serious ethical and political issues inhere in human action. If we are to be true to our never fully realized potential for ethical responsibility—or if we are to survive as a unique species— we must draw on the funded experience of man's history as a conscious, self-critical being. We must also look ahead, as best we can, in our utterly novel situation in which we face ultimate limits to growth (Meadows, Meadows, Randers, & Behrens, 1972), with the closing of the global frontier and our dawning realization that, willy-nilly, mankind shares a common fate.

In discussing future prospects and challenges with respect to psychology and ethics, I will approach the future, which is most uncertain, by way of the present, which we think we know. As for the present, I will review some ethical issues that arise in each of the four roles encompassing the activities of psychologists: research, human services, public policy, and teaching. The issues that I highlight are ones that I expect to be with us for at least the short-term future. I will then speculate about some issues for which I think we should be readying ourselves.

My comments on ethical issues connected with the psychologist's research role are brief, since the extensive report of the Cook committee is readily available. I focus rather on what might be seen as an emerging new commandment, formulated by Rommetweit (1972) in a discussion of European philosophy of the social sciences: Thou shalt not seek knowledge about thine Brother that cannot be converted into self-insight in Him. This commandment sets supreme value upon the integrity of human beings as conscious actors and forbids the acquisition of knowledge that can be used manipulatively. While the statement is extreme and Rommetweit regards it as unworkable, it brings into focus an ethical concern that is widely shared. People can be treated as objects of research, in this view, only insofar as what is learned adds *directly* to their resources as subjects. (It is odd how the term "subject" or S has reversed its connotation in the current psychological literature—so markedly that the Cook committee replaced it with the term "participant." From a researcher's standpoint, the human subject *is* an object.)

One can agree wholeheartedly that it is desirable for psychological science to add to people's resources for self-understanding—and even argue that one of the basic justifications of the psychological enterprise is that collectively, in the long run, it tends toward this end—while still regarding it as undesirable to forbid any inquiry that cannot have this result. As Rommetweit points out, any application of the principle to actual decisions about whether or not to undertake particular research with particular people must presuppose foreknowledge of what can be communicated to the subject and understood by him. Such knowledge is often unavailable, and one readily thinks of instances (for example, research with infants or young children, or with the mentally retarded, or with the severely disturbed) where what is learned from research cannot be converted to self-insight yet is surely of value to those charged with the subject's nurture or care, to the subject's benefit. The commandment as stated converts a positive ideal—the enhancement of the other's humanity —into a negative proscription: research that does not contribute directly toward achieving the ideal must not be undertaken. The former is acceptable, not the latter. A humane scientific psychology needs more complex, less restrictive ethical guidance.

That, in Francis Bacon's phrase, "Knowledge is power" gives rise to ethical dilemmas even in the human sciences where knowledge is faulty and fragmentary. A generation disenchanted with power for whom science and its rationalism have lost their mystique finds it easy to think of placing whole areas of inquiry off limits. Given man's intrinsic dependence on knowledge, that would be a sad mistake. We should rather focus our ethical concerns on the humane and respectful treatment of the research participant and on the uses to which our psychological knowledge is put—a matter we next consider.

It is in regard to the applications of psychology to human service —in regard to psychology as a profession—that ethical issues were first considered explicitly in the discipline. The traditional ways of maintaining ethical practice in American clinical psychology face some perplexing challenges in a day of encounter groups and nude marathons, of wildly democratized psychotherapeutic fads in which a randomly drawn undergraduate may well turn out to fancy himself a Gestalt therapist. These problems may be practically troublesome, but they do not raise fundamental new ethical issues. They speak to what is evidently a deep felt "vitamin lack," in some strata of contemporary society, that must somehow be assuaged whether under responsible professional auspices or not. Underlying the confusions that this cultural malaise entails are some serious ethical perplexities.

One perplexing situation arises from the crisis of confidence that clinical (and community) psychology shares with the other helping professions; the effectiveness of its helping techniques is questionable. Outcome research on psychotherapy is out of style because of its dismally unimpressive findings. To a greater extent than we like to admit, psychotherapy is not an applied science; with the important partial exception of the behavior therapies, it is an art little connected with established scientific principles and only weakly supported by evidence. Is its practice ethical? In an era sensitized to the perspective of cost-effectiveness, one has qualms.

Without wishing to provide a reassuring answer too quickly, I do not want to leave the matter defined wholly in terms of cost/effectiveness. Human suffering, anxiety, self-doubt, estrangement, and guilt have always been with us. People need somewhere to turn for comfort, reassurance, and attentive communication; when their traditional recourses are unavailable or unsatisfying for whatever reason, new professions arise to fill the void. If the new professions "cure," so much the better; perhaps it may be enough that they *care*. The ethical problems of responsible and professionalized caring are well known to the priesthood. This function has been adopted from the priesthood by the mental-health professions.

But the priestly role is a risky model for a profession that also regards itself as an applied science. Another aspect of the role—the prescriptive one—seems to put the mental-health practitioner in a dubious ethical position. What is the good life, and how ought man to live? Once the traditional and theological answers are no longer taken for granted and people are left on their own to make the choice, they may turn for guidance to the mental-health professional as a scientific guru. But science knows little more than "scientology" about these matters. Psychological science can develop contingent knowledge about the consequences and side effects of particular value choices or about the conditions under which particular values can best be realized. In uncovering covert processes such as rationalization or displacement, psychology can suggest more stringent criteria of authenticity than were previously common. In tracing the interconnections that tie together the various facets of a syndrome like authoritarianism, it can enrich or complicate the context of choice for child-rearing and living. But psychology can only describe and elaborate upon human ends, not prescribe them. Psychologists risk becoming inauthentic themselves if they accept in the name of science the guru image that is so readily projected upon them.

To view the helper's role in this way is to regard a *collaborative* relationship as ethically preferable to either a prescriptive or a manipulative one. The ideal is a coequal relationship between mutually respecting and caring persons. But it is intrinsic to helping relationships, be they parental or educational or therapeutic, that they are asymmetrical, not fully mutual. The helper is in at least some respects wiser or more experienced or more competent or less upset than the helped; that is why his help is sought. The practical ethics of helping requires the helper to plan and guide his part in the relationship in order to increase its mutuality, in order to enhance the competence of the helped to participate as an equal and make the choices that are right for him. Entrenched dependency is the pitfall. Skill in so conducting a relationship is not spontaneous; it is a discipline that must be learned. That does not mean that we need to condemn it as manipulative. Outright manipulation, as in the behavior therapies, seems warranted, under careful safeguards, to the extent that the helped are beyond the reach of collaboration (as in the case of autistic or mentally retarded children) or to the extent that the client can in effect be made a collaborator in the manipulative process (as in symptom-oriented behavior modification).

The service contexts upon which I have touched center on individual helping relationships, whereas the psychological professional who serves an institution—a school system, a hospital, an army, a business, or a prison—faces other problems to which we have become sensitive. Institutions have their own purposes, which may not coincide with the interests of each of their members or with those of other citizens. And institutions differ in their resources, their power to command the services of professional psychologists. When psychologists are available to industry and government but not to the poor, the situation is ethically troubling.

Applied psychologists who work in such institutional contexts must often steer their way through complex ethical shoals. We are aware of the opprobrium suffered by military psychology in the eyes of many during the Vietnam war. As individual psychologists, we naturally have different answers concerning the conditions under which it is ethical for us to participate. I see no general solution to the problem, but perhaps it may help to view it in a broader context. The ethical difficulties that confront applied psychology hinge on its embeddedness in inequity and injustice in the environing society. To the extent that psychologists as citizens can join effectively with their fellows in reducing inequities and correcting injustice, the ethical dilemmas entailed in their participation in established social institutions are mitigated. Here ethics and politics merge, and we come to the ethical problems associated with psychology's participation in public policy.

Currently, in the sphere of public policy, psychologists who are concerned with human welfare cannot help being so preoccupied with political frustration that ethical issues hardly come to the fore.

As this is written early in the second Nixon term, it is not a time when government listens to our voice as psychologists, and as citizens we are too few to be taken seriously as a political force. As we register to our dismay the drastic retrenchment in the national commitment to human welfare, our mood tends toward impotent rage—understandable, to be sure, but not impressive either ethically or politically.

In what we can hope is a political off-season, it is through our previous works, particularly the testing movement, that our influence is most felt. Here psychologists are involved in dilemmas that are at once ethical, political, and technical-scientific. A technology that we developed in the service of equal opportunity on the basis of individual merit is widely seen as a bulwark of the existing social hierarchy, a bastion of "institutional racism" that pins self-confirming labels on people, especially children and youth, in order to perpetuate the cleavage between haves and have-nots (see Smith, 1969).

This is not the occasion to examine the tangled issues concerning the substantial element of truth in this charge, and the dubious alternatives that are available to the use of tests. I would like to suggest, however, that the testing movement in psychology has unwittingly contributed to the prevalence of a unidimensional scale of merit that is applied to both individuals and institutions. Johnny, IQ 140, is better than Mary, IQ 115, who is better than Juan, IQ 95. In the same vein, Harvard is better than Ohio State, which is better than Podunk State, which in turn is superior to Centerville Community College (see Jencks & Riesman, 1968). In this case, selectivity is the criterion. Widespread commitment to such a preemptive evaluative dimension is humanly damaging. Perversely, the more reliable and valid our assessment of people and of educational institutions, the more damaging is our assessment to the self-respect of those who fall short on the single scale of merit, and to mutually respectful relations among people and institutions that know one another's placement on it. We are preserved—to the extent that we are—by the technical deficiencies of our evaluative procedures!

Psychologists would do well to be less defensive about the IQ, which is a practical index of real but limited value, and more concerned about contributing, if they can, to an evaluative perspective that balances a wider variety of loosely linked dimensions. Who, except narrow academics, would seriously argue that the IQ exhausts the range of valued human qualities, talents, and virtues, or for that matter, that it predicts much besides *academic* performance—except crudely? Our rapid progress toward nearly universal higher education that is probably loosening the previous tight linkage between educational attainment and subsequent occupational prestige (with some attendant confusion and personal disappointment) gives us a first chance to loosen the stranglehold that the unidimensional evaluative schema has had upon us.

As I focus on psychology's teaching role, I am concerned not with the student-teacher relationship, which indeed has its ethical problems, but with psychological education in the broadest sense—with the psychology we give away to our students and to the public at large, which, Miller (1969) thinks, is our most substantial contribution to human welfare. From an ethical perspective, the most important aspect of psychology we give away is the image of man that we convey explicitly or implicitly, the assumptions about man's potentialities and limitations, and about his relations to the meaningful world of resposible human action and to the natural-science world of energy transformations and blind causation. The image of man that we purvey is important because man is a uniquely reflective creative. He has beliefs about himself as an individual and as a species; individually and collectively, he has knowledge about his past and expectations about his future. All these beliefs and expectations enter as determinants of human choice and human action. So it matters what man believes about himself. Psychology as a vastly popular academic subject has much to say that bears upon man's self-perception. For a teaching psychologist (and in one way or another we are all teachers), a first step toward responsibility is to realize that most of what we have to say concerning our image of man is metapsychology—a matter of prior assumptions or stipulations that constitute the very terms of psychological fact—not of empirical, evidential, scientific conclusions. We need to examine the psychology that we are giving away from this perspective.

B. F. Skinner's (1971) best-seller *Beyond Freedom and Dignity* provides a convenient target for my ethical concerns since it caricatures the positivist tradition that has been the mainstream of American behavioristic psychology. The book is virtually pure metapsychology, 190 proof, and it appalls me in spite of my respect for Skinner's great scientific and technological contributions. Skinner's metapsychology that denies human freedom and dignity is stipulated a priori, not established empirically. And it has ethical consequences. As Arthur Koestler put it humorously over the BBC (*The Listener*, February 22, 1973), "If you tell an American college undergraduate that he is nothing but on overgrown rat, obeying the same laws as the rat obeys in the Skinner box, he will grow into an overgrown rat and grow whiskers and bite your finger." Or, more seriously, he may be likely to assume a manipulative rather than mutual relationship to his fellows, and he may be less likely to attempt responsible ethical choice as he faces his own future and that of mankind. Cumulated across many undergraduates and the reading public, the likely effects can make an important difference. I am trying to counteract them!

Of course an alternative metapsychology is possible, more in accord with human experience than Skinner's and equally compatible with a scientific psychology—indeed more so, since it makes fewer dogmatic exclusions. Chien (1972) contributes substantially to its basis, and I have attempted elsewhere (Smith, 1974) to elaborate upon and and promulgate it.

Having sampled some of the ethical problems that are raised by psychology's present roles, we can look toward the future. For the immediate future, the old weatherman's best prediction probably holds: tomorrow's weather will be like today's. As we look ahead, the grim question of whether there is to be any future at all arises. Bewteen the Cassandra prophets of doom and our own natural tendency to bury our heads in the sand when faced with ominous uncertainty, it is particularly hard for us to think constructively about the distant future (see Smith, 1973a).

John Platt (1971), the polymath biophysicist-futurologist, has helped me to get my own head straight in thinking about the future by breaking it down into three segments: the *ballistic* future where a modified "weatherman's prediction" of projected trends holds because causal processes that are presently underway cannot feasibly be deflected; the conditional, *if-then* future in which predictions hinge intelligibly on human decisions and actions that are presently open to us; and the *guesswork* future of prophecy and of positive or negative Utopias, in which the chain of if-then contingencies becomes so complex that no deterministic or even probabilistic prediction can sensibly be made on an evidential basis. Obviously, these three futures are not fixed segments of the calendar: the cuts in time are placed differently for different aspects of different issues. In the small world of our personal lives, the three segments march in rapid sequence. In the larger world of public policy, the time scale is necessarily broader. Projections of future population growth, for example, are ballistically fixed within definable limits well into the twenty-first century by the present age structure of the population and weatherman predictions about death rates. (The relativity of Platt's distinction—its heuristic rather than substantive status—is illustrated by the fact that a genocidal nuclear world war could upset the ballistic prediction. If we entertain *this* contingency, the whole future slips into the if-then category.)

This tripartite schematization of the future helps us to organize our practical thinking in ways that are relevant to ethical issues. In the ballistic future, all we can do is adapt or adjust. Our coping, of course, can be more or less intelligent and effective, more or less attentive to the long-term context in which our options are open. The prophetic future is the terrain in which we can exercise our imagination with Utopian thinking, which can be useful to us so long as it does not lull us into carelessness or scare us into desperation and apathy. Psychologists could contribute much more than they do to the formulation of human goals were they to project more Utopias that incorporate their psychological assumptions and knowledge. That Skinner (1948) set an example for us in his book *Walden Two* is to his great credit, whatever one thinks of his model of a desirable future (I do not like it).

It is the intermediate future of if-then contingency that deserves our closest attention, as the segment in which present human decision and action can settle our fates one way or another. It is here that contingent knowledge, the stock-in-trade of science, can be brought effectively to bear.

My complaint about much futurological speculation is that the projected trend lines of which it is so fond neglect the tripartite distinction. I am thinking of those familiar exponential curves that tend to end in absurdities—for instance, the entire American population belonging to the American Psychological Association by the turn of the century (that was E. G. Boring's straight-faced extrapolation) or the death of the human enterprise in a chaos of overpopulation, pollution, and the depletion of energy resources. These are prophecies rather than scientific if-then predictions. If we misunderstand them in the ballistic mode, we are as likely to be paralyzed by them as mobilized to disconfirm them—clearly the intent of the more apocalyptic predictors (see, for example, Meadows et al., 1972) who envision themselves as voicing a self-disconfirming prophecy on the model of predictions of traffic fatalities by the National Safety Council before each major holiday weekend.

One of my main complaints about the prevalent popular metapsychologies, positivistic *and* humanistic, that psychologists are most conspicuously giving away to the attentive public is that their models of man provide little place or support for man as a planner for this middle-range future in which our fates are decided by our present actions or inactions. I agree with Skinner (speaking at the University of Michigan, April 20, 1973) that man's fate is currently in the balance and that deliberate planning, using all the resources of science including scientific psychology, is needed if we are to avert catastrophe. But Skinner's positivistic metapsychology of environmental determinism—his input-output analysis with an empty organism (the black box)—leaves no place for the citizen-planner. Frazier, the benign technocrat of *Walden Two*, enters as a deus ex machina. So, for that matter, does Skinner himself; there is no place for the creative scientist in Skinner's system. Skinner's official model of man, if we believe in it, deprives us of the freedom, dignity, and ethical responsibility that we need if we are to shape our conditional future toward human ends.

As for the popular versions of the humanistic psychology linked to the sensitivity-training and encounter-group movement (Back, 1972), they have been so preoccupied with reaction against the dehumanized rationality of positivistic science and technology that, in the spirit of romantic escapism, they encourage people to neglect the real contingencies on which our future depends. Turning on the here and now may be a therapeutic corrective that is useful to self-alienated victims of an unsuccessful search for meaning in modern life; in man's present predicament, however, it could spell disaster as an enduring posture. As an *alternative* culture, the so-called counterculture with which humanistic psychology resonates enriches the dimensions of modern life. As a *successor* culture, it could be suicidal.

A variety of challenges crowd into view, with ethical issues attached to each, if we focus on the intermediate future, which can be either menacing or promising depending upon what we decide to do about it. Thanks to the scientific fruit of the tree of knowledge, we can no longer blame our present and prospective misfortunes on acts of God. In most emerging problems, human behavior is the stumbling block. Such familiar problems, each potentially solvable in the contingent future but each an interlinked source of potential disaster, are the control of nuclear armaments, the world population crisis (especially acute in the impoverished "developing" countries), environmental pollution and the disruption of life-sustaining ecosystems, and—now coming into view—the energy crisis that results from the American habit, formed on the reckless frontier, of squandering resources. Because these problems have been the subject of much sophisticated discussion in the public domain, I bypass them in favor of three others where public attention and concern is needed. None of these problems can be considered the private property of psychology, yet each has its psychological ingredients. Difficult ethical issues lurk near the core of all three.

The first problem, one special to the United States and the industrialized countries, concerns the enormous disparities that exist between our sector of the world and the rest of it. From a ballistic perspective based on intransigent facts that can hardly be altered sufficiently to reverse current trends in the near future, these disparities are almost bound to increase. Do what we can, we of the haves are likely to face before long an overpopulated, underfed world of have-nots in which periodic famines rage and life deteriorates Calcutta-style. We cannot conceive of raising this impoverished world to anything like our present (and ever-expanding) rate of energy expenditure; even if an inexhaustible source of nuclear energy should become available, I am told that to do so might raise world temperatures to a level that would disrupt the supports of life as we know it. How are we to orient ourselves to such a world of poverty and extreme distress? The concept of Christian charity suggests an ethical solution—voluntarily beginning to reduce our expenditures of energy and resources, while assisting the poorer countries toward a level of material life equal to our own. Such a prospect in keeping with Christian ethics will probably seem to you (as it does to me) less likely than the prospect of our hardening our hearts, building a figurative Chinese Wall around our affluence, and attempting to brazen it out, perhaps with imperialist military ventures and the support of client-nations. The prospect frightens me, as a civilization that is "saved" in such a way is surely lost. Our democratic freedoms would receive short shrift. Perhaps in the trauma of Vietnam and its sequelae we are experiencing a foretaste of what may befall us if we do not prevent such an outcome and choose a better fate for ourselves and others.

The basic ethical problem is one for all, not especially for psychology. The problem is acute for the official Catholic Church, given its stand on matters affecting the population issue. For psychology, the present ethical relevance is a matter of priorities. Some of us can already see this potentially grim future looming on the horizon. The challenge, in our research, our teaching, and our representations with respect to public policy is to mobilize our commitment and our competence toward the prohuman alternative while there is still time. Optimists like myself by temperament can find some cause for taking heart in the small but increasing stream of psychological research on altruism (for example, Macaulay & Berkowitz, 1970), which has begun to compete with our long research preoccupation with hostility and aggression. Perhaps more important is the emergence of a new quasi-religious concern for man's unity with nature, in which the old American shibboleth "The bigger the better" is coming to be seen as the cultural aberration that it clearly is. Psychologists are only beginning to interest themselves in this potentially crucial change in our value system.

A related problem and challenge, which will be exacerbated by the pressures to be expected in connection with my first problem, concerns what we are to do, nationally and internationally, about the cultural identity and interdependence of peoples in a shrinking world. A generation ago when the old colonialism was collapsing, we could be more optimistic than seems possible today. As we presently look about us, we see a world of new and mutually hostile nationalisms, and a society of our own in which submerged groups (for example, the Indians, of whom very few white Americans had previously been aware as *people*) are clamoring, sometimes violently, for recognition and for equity that seems entirely beyond their grasp. The ethical, the political, and I should think also the aesthetic desirability of some kind of cultural pluralism seems increasingly obvious to many of us. Psychologists, fortunately no longer entirely white ones, are inevitably drawn into the fray. The issues become entangled with the problems of IQ and test technology, touched upon earlier, where some psychologists act as though they have a vested interest in the unidimensional evaluative schema that I earlier deplored.

For psychologists of whatever ethnic identity, the special ethical problem in this area seems to be how to maintain scientific and intellectual integrity and, at the same time, compassionate respect for people from other groups, in dealing with issues close to people's sense of identity and selfhood. There has been a good deal of understandable but regrettable foolishness perpetrated on all sides.

A third problem that strikes me as more serious than liberal psychologists realize, concerns authority, or law and order in the current debased phrasing. Hobbesian social philosophy becomes reinvented as Hobbesian features of disorder and violence rise to prominence in the contemporary social world. Psychologists on their part assume that they have laid the topic of authoritarianism to rest, when they have merely abandoned it. Little has been done with Erich Fromm's (1941) valuable early concept of rational authority. Much more than sociologists, psychologists seem intellectually and morally uncomfortable in this area of concern. Meanwhile, the steady long-term attrition of arbitrary traditional authority—be it in church, state, school, or family—seems beyond question, as is the fact that the relative vacuum of legitimate authority has ensued, together with the rapid rate of change in these matters, has left severe social problems in its wake. My fear is that unless we cope adequately with the basis of social order, drastic antidemocratic, antihuman solutions may be sought successfully by some and imposed upon the rest of us. While I far from bemoan the passing of traditional authority, I think it urgent to explore viable alternative patterns. The challenge to psychology is to contribute ideas and evidence to this venture. Again, the issues are difficult in part because they are value laden and readily become ideological.

Perhaps you wonder why I did not put at the head of my list one popular topic that I have not mentioned: the control of the mind. The reason is that this topic does not strike me as a priority matter. I think a lot of poppycock has been said about it, from the false alarm about subliminal perception in the service of "hidden persuaders" (would that *all* advertising were subliminal!) to the furor about brainwashing (a drastic process that is real enough, but no Pavlovian mystery) to the proposal of drugs for pacifying aggressive presidents and the dramatic report of electrically wired bulls programmed to stop a charge in their tracks. Humanists have taken inflated newspaper speculations at face value, and are running scared—when they leave off pooh-poohing scientific psychology.[2]

As a citizen, I am concerned with the monopolistic control of the media by crass materialistic commercialism, and I am alarmed when the president appears to take lightly the traditional liberties of the press. I think the public often is manipulated, but the manipulation that I fear takes quite traditional forms, applied with more potent technical resources and perhaps with greater ruthlessness. In spite of the mystique encouraged by psychologists in the advertising industry, I do not think that psychology possesses much special knowledge that is readily converted into this kind of power. No psychologists were called upon to assist in Watergate.

We know enough about the incredible complexity of the electrochemical processes and related neural structures that somehow underlie human experience and action to make the wise guess that in the foreseeable future our advances in understanding this complexity will be gains in understanding in *principle* rather than in full actuality. I am not afraid, short of the remote future of positive or negative Utopias, that memories or compulsions will be implanted in us by wiring us up or feeding us RNA. Neither am I afraid that Skinner's strategies and tactics of behavior modification will be used to shape our actions according to somebody else's pleasure. In the limited but important spheres in which Skinner's strategies have been effective, I attribute their success as much to the general common sense and psychological acumen of the applied Skinnerians as to the power of Skinnerian theory. My concern with Skinner is with the bemusing effect that his speculative metapsychology may have on us, not with the insidious power of his scientific theory and techniques.

Psychology that takes ethics seriously has a fundamental challenge to contribute in understanding and in professional practice to the development of people who, in interdependence, are capable of taking charge of their lives and shaping their future in accordance with emerging requirements of human nature. In this continuing interac-

---

[2] But see Valenstein (1973) for a searching review of the use of brain surgery for behavioral control—a worrisome and irresponsible development that does indeed pose serious ethical problems.

tive and dialectical process, human nature itself will be modified, as will the human situation. Short of disaster, there is no visible end to this process, no equivalent to the Marxist's classless society or to the traditional Catholic eschatology as a stated goal. But I would not wish an end to history. I prefer the continually advancing contingent future that can be shaped by human action to Utopia or the Heavenly City.

I conclude this essay on what should be the concern of the ethical psychologist by referring again to John Platt. After reviewing what he regarded as the extraordinary unprecedented threats that mankind faces, which also represent opportunities if man can overcome them, Platt (1966) suggests, in a grand image, that if we *somehow* surmount the crises that lie before us, our human nature will be qualitatively transformed, just as our primate forebears became protopeople through tool using and speech and our savage ancestors were transformed to peasants and city dwellers by the invention of agriculture. Platt spoke of this hoped-for transformation as the step to man, the title of his book. Platt is not a psychologist, and he left the nature of the transformation that he heralded a mystery. For a psychology that is both humanistic *and* scientific, I can think of no greater challenge than to contribute to understanding and bringing about this step. Our future depends upon it.

BIBLIOGRAPHY

Ad Hoc Committee on Ethical Standards in Psychological Research. *Ethical principles in the conduct of research with human participants.* Washington, D.C. American Psychological Association, 1973.

Back, K. *Beyond words. The story of sensitivity training and the encounter movement.* New York: Russell Sage, 1972.

Chein, I. *The science of behavior and the image of man.* New York: Basic Books, 1972.

Fromm, E. *Escape from freedom.* New York: Holt, Rinehart and Winston, 1941.

Jencks, C., & Riesman, D. *The academic revolution.* New York: Doubleday, 1968.

Macaulay, J., & Berkowitz, L. (Eds.) *Altruism and helping behavior.* New York: Academic, 1970.

Maslow, A. H. *The farther reaches of human nature.* New York: Viking, 1971.

May, R. *Power and innocence: A search for the sources of violence.* New York: Norton, 1972.

Mead, G. H. *Mind, self, and society.* Chicago: University of Chicago Press, 1934.

Meadows, D. G., Meadows, D. L. Randers, J., & Behrens, W. W. *The limits to growth.* New York: Universe Books, 1972.

Miller, G. A. *Mind, self, and society.* Chicago: University of Chicago Press, 1934.

Meadows, D. G., Meadows, D. L., Randers, J., & Behrens, W. W. *The limits to grow.* New York: Universe Books, 1972.

Miller, G. A. Psychology as a means of promoting human welfare. *American Psychologist,* 1969, **24**, 1063–1075.

Platt, J. *The step to man.* New York: Wiley, 1966.

Platt, J. How men can shape their future. *Futures,* 1971, **3** (1), 32–47.

Rommetweit, R. Language games, syntactic structures and hermeneutics. In J. Israel & H. Tajfel (Eds.), *The context of social psychology: A critical assessment.* New York and London: Academic, 1972.

Skinner, B. F. *Walden two.* New York: Macmillan, 1948.

Skinner, B. F. *Beyond freedom and dignity.* New York: Knopf, 1971.

Smith, M. B. Racism, education, and student protest. *Illinois School Journal,* 1969, **49**, 207–214.

Smith, M. B. Environmental degradation and human behavior: Can psychology help? *Representative Research in Social Psychology,* 1973a, **4**, 227–234.

Smith, M. B. Is psychology relevant to new priorities? *American Psychologist,* 1973b, **28**, 463–471.

Smith, M. B. *Humanizing social psychology.* San Francisco: Jossey-Bass, 1974.

Valenstein, E. S. *Brain control. A critical examination of brain stimulation and psychosurgery.* New York: Wiley-Interscience, 1973.

CHAPTER 2

The Insights of the Judaeo-Christian Tradition and the Development of an Ethical Code

Richard A. McCormick, S.J.
Georgetown University
Washington, D.C.

I am delighted to have been invited to address you on the subject assigned to me. It has been said that medicine is too important to be left to doctors alone. The same is usually true of theology. It is too important to be left to theologians alone. And I believe that psychology is too important to be left to psychologists alone. All disciplines are aware of their intersecting and interdisciplinary character in our time. Theologians have recently become aware of their deep reliance on disciplines other than their own. The topic assigned to me indicates a confidence among you that there is perhaps something that psychology can wrest from theological reflection. I think that is true, but I tremble to have my remarks made the measure of this point.

The title of this paper would be more accurate if it read: how one individual in the Judaeo-Christian tradition sees the relevance of this tradition for the development of a code of ethics in professional psychology. There is an acknowledged pluralism of theologies and methods in contemporary moral reflection and no one individual can speak with assurance for a whole fraternity. Furthermore, when speaking of the "Judaeo-Christian tradition" one must locate himself carefully. The continuity of the Old and New Testaments, and the broad coincidence of value judgments in both certainly justify the usage "Judaeo-Christian." My emphasis, however, will fall on the term "Christian" since I would not presume to speak for a contemporary dimension with which I am not personally familiar.

Let me begin by saying that to determine the insights of the Judaeo-Christian tradition on the development of an ethical code in psychology, we must treat two major themes. First, we must see what a code is and how it is developed. A code is, I take it, the conclusion of a process. We must lift up, therefore, those things that go into this process to see at what point a religious tradition might exert its influence. I hope to make it clear that the Judaeo-Christian tradition does indeed influence a code of ethics, but only at a certain point in the developmental process that issues in a code, and only in a carefully restricted way. Second, we must determine the meaning of the Judaeo-Christian tradition and how it influences morals in general. This will reveal, I hope, how it may be expected to influence the specific matter of a code for professional psychologists.

HOW A CODE IS DEVELOPED

A code is the concretization in a certain sphere of more general moral convictions or postures. Hence to see how the Judaeo-Christian tradition influences the development of a code, we must first see how moral positions arise and are maintained. This is a huge and wearying undertaking and I can do no more here than suggest the barest outlines of one approach to this question.

The first thing to be said is that moral convictions do not originate from rational analyses or arguments. Let us take slavery as an example. We do not hold that slavery is humanly demeaning and immoral chiefly because we have argued to this rationally. Rather, first our sensitivities are sharpened to the meaning and value of human persons. We then *experience* the out-of-jointness, inequality, and injustice of slavery. We then *judge* it to be wrong. At this point we develop "arguments" to criticize, modify, and above all communicate this judgment. Reflective analysis is an attempt to reinforce rationally, communicably, and from other sources what we grasp at a different level. Discursive reflection does not *discover* the good but only *analyzes* it. The good that reason seems to discover is the good that was already hidden in the original intuition.[1]

This needs more explanation. How do we arrive at definite moral obligations, prescriptions, and proscriptions? How does the general thrust of our persons toward good and away from evil become concrete, even as concrete as a code of do's and don't's, and caveats? It happens somewhat as follows—and in this I am following closely the school of J. de Finance, G. de Broglie, G. Grisez, John Finnis, and others. We proceed by asking what are the goods or values man can seek, the values that define his human opportunity, his flourishing? We can answer this by examining man's basic tendencies. For it is impossible to act without having an interest in the object, and it is impossible to be attracted by, to have interest in something without some inclination already present. What then are the basic inclinations?

With no pretense at being exhaustive, we could list some of the following as basic inclinations present prior to acculturation: the tendency to preserve life; the tendency to mate and raise children; the tendency to explore and question; the tendency to seek out other men and obtain their approval—friendship; the tendency to establish good relations with unknown higher powers; the tendency to use intelligence in guiding action; the tendency to develop skills and exercise them in play and the fine arts. In these inclinations our intelligence spontaneously and without reflection grasps the possibilities to which they point, and prescribes them. Thus we form naturally and without reflection the basic principles of practical or moral reasoning. Or as philosopher John Finnis (1970) renders it:

> What is spontaneously understood when one turns from contemplation to action is not a set of Kantian or neo-scholastic "moral principles" identifying this as right and that as wrong, but a set of values which can be expressed in the form of principles such as "life is a good-to-be-pursued and realized and what threatens it is to be avoided [p. 373].

---

[1] The following remarks are drawn from Finnis (1970).

We have not yet arrived at a determination of what concrete actions are morally right or wrong; but we have laid the basis. Since these basic values are equally basic and irreducibly attractive, the morality of our conduct is determined by the adequacy of our openness to these values. For each of these values has its self-evident appeal as a participation in the unconditioned Good we call God. The realization of these values in intersubjective life is the only adequate way to love and atttain God.

Further reflection by practical reason tells us what it means to remain open and to pursue these basic human values. First, we must take them into account in our conduct. Simple disregard of one or other shows we have set our mind against this good. Second, when we can do so as easily as not, we should avoid acting in ways that inhibit these values, and prefer ways that realize them. Third, we must make an effort on their behalf when their realization in another is in extreme peril. If we fail to do so, we show that the value in question is not the object of our efficacious love and concern. Finally, we must never choose directly against a basic good. When one of the irreducible values falls immediately under our choice, to choose against it in favor of some other basic value is arbitrary, for all such values are equally basic and self-evidently attractive. What is to count as "turning against a basic good" is, of course, the crucial moral question. My only point here is that particular moral judgments are incarnations of these more basic normative positions, which have their roots in spontaneous, prereflective inclinations.

Even though these inclinations can be identified as prior to acculturation, still they exist as culturally conditioned. We tend toward values as perceived. And the culture in which we live shades our perception of values. Philip Rieff in *The Triumph of the Therapeutic* notes that a culture survives by the power of institutions to influence conduct with "reasons" that have sunk so deeply into the self that they are implicitly understood—"the unwitting part of it" as Harry Stack Sullivan puts it.[2] In other words, decisions are made, policies set not chiefly by articulated norms, codes, regulations, and philosophies, but by "reasons" that lie below the surface. This is the dynamic aspect of a culture, and in this sense the moral problems of psychol-

---

[2] These reflections are borrowed from Callahan (1972).

ogy are cultural. Our way of perceiving the basic human values and relating to them is shaped by our whole way of looking at the world.

Let me take an example from another area of concern, that of bioethics. In relating to the basic human values several images of man are possible, as Callahan (1972) has observed. First, there is a power-plasticity model. In this model, nature is alien, independent of man, possessing no inherent value. It is capable of being used, dominated, and shaped by man. Man sees himself as possessing an unrestricted right to manipulate in the service of his goals. Death is something to be overcome, outwitted. Second, there is the sacral-symbiotic model. In its religious forms, nature is seen as God's creation, to be respected and heeded. Man is not the master; he is the steward and nature is a trust. In secular forms, man is seen as a part of nature. If man is to be respected, so is nature. We should live in harmony and balance with nature. Nature is a teacher, showing us how to live with it. Death is one of the rhythms of nature, to be gracefully accepted.

The model which seems to have "sunk deep" and shaped our moral imagination and feelings—shaped our perception of basic values—is the power-plasticity model. We are, corporately, *homo technologicus*. The best solution to the dilemmas created by technology is more technology. We tend to eliminate the maladapted condition (defectives, retardates, and so on) rather than adjust the environment to it. Even our language is sanatized and shades from view our relationship to basic human values. We speak of "surgical air strikes" and "terminating a pregnancy," ways of blunting the moral imagination from the shape of our conduct. My only point here is that certain cultural "reasons" qualify or shade our perception of and our grasp on the basic human values. Thus these reasons are the cultural soil of our moral convictions and have a good deal to say about where we come out when a code is concerned.

Once the basic values are identified along with their cultural tints and trappings, we attempt in a disciplined rational way to develop "middle axioms" or mediating principles. These relate the basic values to concrete choice. The major problem any professional ethic faces is to reinterpret the concrete demands of the basic values in new circumstances without forfeiting its grasp on these values.

This is what I take to be the process whereby a code of professional ethics is generated.

JUDAEO-CHRISTIAN INFLUENCE ON THE DEVELOPMENT OF A CODE OF ETHICS FOR PSYCHOLOGISTS

There are undoubtedly those who grow nervous and apprehensive at the thought of a religious influence on professional codes. This is most likely traceable to a misunderstanding. At least very many psychologists might conjure up the picture of a theologian citing a text from scripture as decisive for clinical practice. Or worse yet, some would see a pope or bishop—supposedly in possession of arcane wisdom that yields solutions to difficult human dilemmas—meddling into an essentially autonomous discipline and telling its practitioners what to do. Even though some theologians remain to a degree biblical fundamentalists, and even though not all hierarchical processes are as rehabilitated to modern times as we would like, these fears are essentially unfounded—precisely because it is almost universally accepted in theological circles that the authoritative sources of Christian tradition (scripture, teaching authority) do not directly translate into independent concrete moral prescriptions and proscriptions. This may come as a surprise to some. I hope it is not a disappointment. To understand why this is so, we must see the meaning of the term "Christian morality."

Christian morality suggests that there is a morality specific to Christians, one that is drawn from Christian sources, and is in principle unavailable to the reasoning of other men, and inapplicable to them. This is not true. Since there is only one destiny possible to all men, there is existentially only one essential morality common to all men, Christians and non-Christians alike. This means that there is a *material* identity between Christian moral demands and those perceivable by reason. Whatever is distinct about Christian morality is found essentially in the style of life, the manner of accomplishing the moral tasks common to all men, not in the tasks themselves. Christian morality is, in its concreteness and materiality, *human* morality. The theological study of morality accepts the human in all its fullness as its starting point. It is the *human* which is then illumined by the person, teaching, and achievement of Jesus Christ. The experience of Jesus is regarded as normative because he is believed to have experienced what it is to be *human* in the fullest way and at the deepest level (McDonagh, 1970). Christian ethics does not and cannot add to human ethical self-understanding as such any material content that is, in principle, strange or foreign to man as he exists and experiences himself.

Therefore, the Judaeo-Christian tradition does not add to the human. Rather it is an outlook on the human, a community of privileged access to the *human*, if you will. The Judaeo-Christian tradition is anchored in faith in the meaning and decisive significance of God's covenant with men, especially as manifested finally in the saving incarnation of Jesus Christ and the revelation of his final coming, his eschatological kingdom which is here aborning but will finally only be given. Faith in these events, love of and loyalty to their central figure, yields a decisive way of viewing and intending the world, of interpreting its meaning, of hierarchizing its values, of reacting to its apparent surds and and conflicts. In this sense the Judaeo-Christian tradition only illumines human values, supports them, provides a context for their reading at given points in history. It aids us in staying human by underlining the truly human against all cultural attempts to distort the human. And it is in this way, I believe, that it exercises its major influence on professional codes—by steadying our gaze on the basic human values that are the parents of more concrete rules and ethical protocols. When we examine several of its key emphases, we will see how they support the human, and we will get some idea of how this tradition exerts its influence on the development of a code.

The Dignity of the Individual Person

The Judaeo-Christian tradition has always seen man as "in relationship to God." This means that man is the bearer of an "alien dignity," a dignity rooting in the value God puts in man. No one has stated this better than Helmut Thielicke (1964):

> This "alien dignity" expresses the fact that it is not man's own worth—his value for producing "good works," his functional proficiency, his pragmatic utility—that gives him his dignity, but rather what God has "spent upon him," the sacrificial love which God has invested in him (Deut. 7:7f). Therefore this alien dignity actualizes itself at the very point where man's own value has become questionable, the point where

his functional value is no longer listed on society's stock market and he is perhaps declared to be "unfit to live" [p. 231].

The greatest affirmation of this alien dignity is, of course, God's Word—become flesh. As Christ is of God, and Christ is *the* man, so all men are God's, his darlings, deriving their dignity from the value He is putting in them. This perspective stands as a profound critique of our tendency to assess man functionally, to weaken our hold on the basic value that is human life. It leads to a particular care for the weakest, most voiceless, voteless, defenseless members of society: orphans, the poor, the aged, the mentally and physically sick, the unborn. All violations of the ethics of experimentation root in and reflect a slipped grasp of man's lovableness, at root an alien lovableness.

It can be persuasively argued, I believe, that the peculiar temptation of a technologically advanced culture such as ours is to view and treat men functionally. Our treatment of the aged is perhaps the sorriest symptom of this. The elderly are probably the most alienated members of our society. "Not yet ready for the world of the dead, not deemed fit for the world of the living, they are shunted aside. More and more of them spend the extra years medicine has given them in 'homes for senior citizens,' in chronic hospitals, in nursing homes—waiting for the end. We have learned how to increase their years, but we have not learned how to help them enjoy their days" (Kass, 1971). Their protest is eloquent because it is helplessly muted and silent. It is a protest against a basically functional assessment of their persons. "Maladaptation" is the term used to describe *them*, rather than the environment. Hence we intervene against the maladapted individual rather than against the environment.

I do not know in detail or by experience the peculiar temptations of psychologists to reproduce in their policies a functional assessment of human beings. But I presume that psychologists are not unlike the rest of men, and therefore have their feet buried deep in a pragmatic culture, and do experience the temptation to use and manipulate generally in terms of that notorious nonpatient, the human race. The Judaeo-Christian tradition will not dictate to you what acts are justifiable, and what are not. It will not give you a code. That is your task and responsibility and risk. But it will insist that there is an ethic of means, because you deal with someone who is of much value than the sum of his parts, someone who is an end-value in all human decisions. That is the way the Judaeo-Christian tradition functions, I think, where the development of a professional code is concerned. It supports our grasp of the basic human values against cultural counterfeits. If you look for more, you will not find it. But if you acknowledge less, you are, I think, in trouble. For a sure grasp on the alien dignity of man is, where a code of ethics is concerned, both very little and very much. It is a kind of compass to steer our deliberations, constrain our eugenic enthusiasms and control our scientific aspirations. But a compass is not a rudder.

The Social Character of the Human Person

If man's dignity is radically in his relationship to God but this is a relationship pursued and matured only through relationships to men, then this relationship to God is unavoidably social. God covenanted with the Jewish *people*, with a group. It was within a group and through a group that the individual was responsible and responsive to God. This is even clearer in the New Testament. "Being in Christ" is a shared existence. Man's new being, of which St. Paul speaks so frequently, is being in a community. Assumption into Christ means assumption into his Body, his People. We cannot exist as Christians except in a community and we cannot define ourselves except as "of a Body." Hence it is Christianly axiomatic that the community of believers (the Church) is the extension of the incarnation. It is similarly axiomatic that those actions wherein we initiate into, fortify, restore, intensify the Christlife (the Christian sacraments) are at once Christ's actions and the actions of the community.

This sense of community, sunk deep into the spontaneous consciousness of Christians, has meant two things to them over the centuries. First, it has meant that my freedom to realize my potentialities as a man is conditioned by the authenticity of the other members of the community, and vice versa. That is, the community exists for the individual. It is not an independent superentity to which we are subordinate, and whose good absorbs our own. It does not serve an abstract ideal; rather that ideal is incarnate in each of its members.

Second, it means that if we cannot exist in isolation, neither can we know as Christians in isolation, and it would be un-Christian to think we do or hope that we could. Our shared knowledge is concerned with God's wonderful saving events and their moral implications. True moral insight, in St. Paul's understanding, is mediated to the individual through participation in the community. Just as the Christian's mode of being is a sharing, so the moral knowledge necessary to its continuation and development is the result of a communal experiece, a communal discernment that prolongs knowledge into the twilight human areas where there are no sharp contours, no bright colors.[3] The Christian is one who spontaneously seeks correction for his own biases within a community of shared loyalty, but of more diverse experience and perspectives.

These two perspectives have enormous implications for moral conduct, and for the protocols of a professional code. I see especially two of major importance. They can only be sketched briefly here. First of all, there is the relation of the individual to the community. Sometimes the individual and the community are conceived as two separable and competing values. The Judaeo-Christian tradition resists this and sees them as co-implicating and interpenetrating each other, as inseparable complementarities. It is not a question of the individual versus the community. We do not harm one for the sake of the other. Harming individuals in a choice or policy is only justifiable to the extent that this individual would himself be exposed to more harm over the long term if such a policy did not exist. Therefore, for instance, if you conclude in a code that it is sometimes legitimate to deceive an individual or expose him to harm, it is only because you have shown clearly that this is the best policy in terms of this individual in the long run. The Judaeo-Christian does not tell us this, but human reason informed by this tradition moves in this direction.

Second, moral knowledge as a community possession and achievement says a good deal about the manner in which a code ought to be developed. Codes developed within a single profession, without the benefit of other competences are very likely to be inadequate. We are learning in the Catholic community that the moral teaching authority of the Church should not be viewed as an isolated club—the hierarchy—in prior possession of the truth. Rather wisdom is resident in the entire community and all must share in the teaching-learning

---

[3] For this emphasis, see for example the many writings of the noted exegete Jerome Murphy-O'Connor, O.P.

process if we are to escape the isolation of our own reflections and if moral stands are to be credible and persuasive. I believe that the Judaeo-Christian tradition suggests something similar for psychologists. Your policies should be the result of a discernment process collaborative in character, involving laymen from a variety of disciplines as partners in the conversation. Thus the tradition functions as a constant corrective against our tendencies toward fragmentation and isolation in the development of moral policies.

Love as the Crowning Human Relationship

When a person is no longer related to other persons, he is quite literally dead. Suicide is the ultimate way of shutting out all other people from one's life. At a time when it is possible to keep lungs breathing and hearts pumping by machine, our attention is refocused on what it means to be human. The answer most frequently given is that to be human means to have a capacity, actually or potentially, for significant human relationships. It is, I believe, not a Christian discovery, but a typically Christian insistence that the crowning achievement of human relationships is love. For St. Paul, love is the epitome of the entire law, the root of other virtues, the bond of perfection, more elevated than all charisms. It is the dominant characteristic of the new mode of being that Paul calls "belonging to Christ," "being in Christ." In the Pauline literature the "old man" is contrasted with the new. The "old man" is characterized by isolation and selfish withdrawal. His traits—all dominantly antisocial—are anger, wrath, malice, slander, dissension, envy, and so on. The "new man's" characteristics are all other-centered: compassion, kindness, lowliness, meekness, patience.

These things are familiar to all of us; but their implications may be easily overlooked. The tradition referred to insists that man's response to God occurs only through relating to others *lovingly*. This is definitive of our growth and maturity as human beings, of the ultimate significance of our lives whatever else they might be. Our actions are good to the extent that they are in their external shape and effects, and their internal motivations, loving. To derogate from this capacity to love, to bypass it, to stultify it is to dehumanize both ourselves and others.

It is this insight which stands behind and illumines the consent canon where experimentation is concerned. Christian ethicians maintain that an individual can become (in carefully delimited circumstances) more fully a person by donation of an organ to another; for by communicating to another of his very being he has more fully integrated himself into the mysterious unity between person and person. Something analogous can be said of experimentation undertaken for the good of others. It can be an affirmation of one's solidarity and Christian concern for others (through the advancement of medicine). Becoming an experimental subject can involve any or all of three things: some degree of risk (at least of complications), pain, associated inconvenience (e.g., prolonging hospital stay, delaying recovery, and so on). To accept these for the good of others could be an act of charitable concern, of genuine love.

While admitting this we have always excluded those incapable of consent from such procedures. Why? Because, I believe, these undertakings become human goods for the donor or subject precisely because and therefore only when they are voluntary; for the personal good under discussion is the good of expressed charity. This demands freedom by its very definition.

The Christian tradition's heavy emphasis on love as the most radical human mandate, reductively the only mandate, necessarily fortifies our grasp on freedom as the highest of instrumental values. All things that attack or subvert man's freedom are violative of the *humanun*. Laws are inherently defensible only because in constricting freedom they actually protect and expand it. There is, it is correctly said, no liberty without law. Codes are nothing more than attempts to set up rules that will guarantee the maximum amount of freedom. All violations of professional ethics are equivalently and reductively encroachments on human freedom.

For instance, misuse of confidential information not only hurts an individual in clinically detectable ways, but in so doing it ultimately restricts his freedom. Similarly, an exorbitant fee-scale in professional work is unethical because it renders the profession less available, thus restricting freedom of access to a needed service. Deception in patient care is an obvious example of diminished freedom.

These are but three recurring emphases in the Judaeo-Christian tradition. There are many more—for example, the sinfulness of man and therefore frequently of his plans and aspirations. Or again, the eschatological view of life and of human ethical action whereby we are led to admit that the final validation and transformation of human effort is given by God with the ultimate coming of His kingdom. These emphases do not yield a code. But they affect it. The stories and symbols that relate the origin of Christianity and nourish the faith of the individual, affect one's perspectives. They sharpen and intensify our focus on the human goods definitive of our flourishing. It is men so informed, men with such "reasons" sunk deep in their being, who face new situations, new dilemmas, and reason together as to what is the best policy, the best protocol for the service of all the values. They do not find concrete answers in their tradition, but they bring a world-view that informs their reasoning—especially by allowing the basic human goods to retain their attractiveness and not be tainted by cultural distortions. This world-view is a continuing check on and challenge to our tendency to make choices in light of cultural enthusiams which sink into and take possession of our unwitting, preethical selves. Such enthusiasms can reduce the good life to mere adjustment in a triumph of the therapeutic; collapse an individual into his functionability; exalt his uniqueness into a lonely individualism or crush it in a suffocating collectivism. In this sense I believe it is true to say that the Judaeo-Christian tradition is much more a value-raiser than an answer-giver. And it affects our values at the spontaneous, pre-thematic level. One of the values inherent in its incarnational ethos is an affirmation of the goodness of man and all about him—including his reasoning and thought processes. The Judaeo-Christian tradition refuses to bypass or supplant human deliberation and hard work in developing ethical protocols within a profession. For that would be blasphemous of the Word of God become human. On the contrary, it asserts their need, but constantly reminds men that what God did and intends for for man is an affirmation of the human and therefore must remain the measure of what man may reasonably decide to do to and for himself.

BIBLIOGRAPHY

Callahan, D. Living with the new biology. *Center Magazine*, 1972, **5**, 4–12.
Finnis, J. M. Natural law and unnatural acts. *Heythrop Journal*, 1970, **11**, 365–387.
Kass, L. R. The new biology: What price relieving man's estate? *Science*, 1971, **174**, 784.

McDonagh, E. Towards a Christian theology of morality. *Irish Theological Quarterly*, 1970, **37**, 187–198.

Rieff, P. *The triumph of the therapeutic: uses of faith after Freud*. New York: Harper and Row, 1966.

Thielicke, H. *The ethics of sex*. New York: Harper and Row, 1964.

CHAPTER 3

Metaethical and Normative Considerations Covering the Treatment of Human Subjects in the Behavioral Sciences[*]

Diana Baumrind

University of California
Berkeley

METAETHICAL AND NORMATIVE CONSIDERATIONS

We are seldom called upon to make the effort of thought required to state our ethical principles, the ordering of these principles, the standards we use to formulate these principles, or the way in which our rules of action and normative judgments follow from these ordered principles and metaethical standards. In asking me to address you today, Dr. Kennedy has in effect called upon me to make such an effort. I, in turn, invite each of you to bring to the forefront of your consciousness the basic tenets of your system of moral philosophy so that the sources of such disagreements as we may have concerning practical ethical judgments on the treatment of human sub-

[*] The author's research referred to in this paper was supported by the National Institute of Child Health and Human Development under Research Grant HD 02228.

jects can be identified. Any system of normative and metaethical rules is based upon a superordinate way of life to which it lends support. If you and I disagree concerning a practical ethical judgment, our disagreement may arise from any of the following causes: (1) a factual disagreement concerning the probable effects of a given action; (2) differences as to how a rule in any given instance should be applied; (3) differences in the relative weights assigned to rules on which we both place a positive value; (4) disagreements as to the direction of value assigned a given rule; (5) different views concerning the nature of good and evil or right and wrong; (6) incompatible theories of justification for moral judgments; and finally (7) fundamental differences in basic world-view and way of life. We must first diagnose the source of difference before we can resolve the disagreement. Differences based upon genuinely contradictory world-views are not resolvable, but there are few of these among people brought up in the same culture. Most differences are resolvable, at least in theory provided that both participants have given some thought to normative and metaethical considerations and are prepared to debate the matter logically and in good faith. I propose to set before you my moral philosophy in those areas which are relevant to practical judgments concerning principles of ethical treatment of human subjects.

I will first present an overview of familiar systems of moral judgment so that I can then characterize my own views in relation to these systems.

Systems of Moral Judgment

Among the world's cultures, there exist systems of moral judgment whose hierarchies of ultimate values are incompatible because their views of the position which the species man occupies in the universe are fundamentally different. In the Judaeo-Christian view, man places himself at the center of the universe:

> And God said, Let us make man in our image, after our likeness: and let him have dominion over the fish of the sea, and over the fowl of the air, and over the cattle, and over all the earth, and over every creeping thing that creepeth upon the earth. . . .
> and God said unto them, Be fruitful, and multiply, and replenish the earth, and subdue it. [Genesis].

Metaethical and Normative Considerations

This view of the position of man in the universe is exclusively Western. It is not shared, for example, by the American Indian, the African, or the Oriental. Nor is it shared by many young people in the United States who believe that all sentient beings are of equal importance and that there is no moral basis for choosing to save a human life over that of another living creature. These young people believe, further, that by subduing the earth, man threatens to destroy it. These contrasting views feature in subjects' responses to two of the Kohlberg (1971) moral dilemma stories.

In brief, the two Kohlberg dilemmas can be paraphrased as follows: a woman is near death from cancer which can only be cured by treatment with a form of radium recently discovered by a druggist in town. He is determined to sell the radium for an exorbitant price which the sick woman's husband, Heinz, cannot afford to pay. The husband cannot raise the money and the druggist will not lower his price. The desperate husband steals the drug for his wife. The subject is asked if Heinz should have stolen the drug, and his responses are probed. In the second story, the drug does not work for Heinz's wife and she wants euthanasia. The subject is asked if the doctor should give her a drug which will make her die.

Here are excerpts from the responses of a devout Christian and a devout Buddhist which demonstrate the contrasting value each places on life and death:

The Christian: "Yes, the man should steal for his wife. A life is worth that. I would penalize the druggist. Wherever there is life there is hope. Even if it only prolonged her life, that would be something. The druggist is trespassing against a higher law than 'Thou Shalt Not Steal.' " Concerning the doctor, the subject says: "I was brought up to believe that the Lord gives and He should be the only one to end it. Thou Shalt Not Kill under any circumstances. The doctor should not give her the drug whether or not the woman wanted it. For an animal, that is different. An animal is not a human. An animal is a luxury for whoever owns it. An animal is not responsible for carrying on civilization or a family."

The Buddhist: "I personally feel that death under certain circumstances and in spite of the fear it produces is not worth violating one's moral essence to avoid. The proscription against stealing is a universal truth, as is accepting one's death. If in any particular case one violates a value judgment, then the truth has no essence. I definitely would not steal for it. I would try to convince my wife to accept her death." Concerning the doctor, the subject says: "Yes, the doctor should give her the drug, she should be able to die as she wishes. We are all part of the universe; we are not bigger and what we do is not more precious than the bird flying or the dog barking. A human life, a dog's life—it is all the same."

I can think of no way by which differences arising from these two world-views could be resolved. Each view facilitates the development of the way of life from which it springs. In the examples given above, my position is closer to that of the Buddhist respondent, although in most of what follows you will detect the Judaic-Christian idealization of man. The high value I place on man is based upon what I perceive to be his unique characteristics. First, man is strongly affected by the symbolic meaning he gives to things and events. To quote von Bertalanffy (1959):

> The monopoly of man is the creation of symbolic universes in language, thought, and all other forms of behavior. . . . Man's unique position in nature is based upon the predominance of symbols in his life [p. 68].

Second, man is consciously concerned with defining his essence. He is not merely conscious, but is in addition self-conscious. Third, man alone, as a function of his self-consciousness, can experience himself as the cause of his purposive actions. That is, man is capable of shaping both his activities and the environment in which these activities occur.

Within the Judaeo-Christian world-view itself there are systems of moral philosophy whose premises are incompatible, such as the systems of Immanuel Kant and John Stuart Mill. According to Kant, the foundation of morality is Good Will. The value of good will resides in itself, not in what it accomplishes. Thus, according to Kant, there is ordinarily no moral significance in preserving life because everyone has a natural inclination to do so. Only when a person desires death and nevertheless, through duty, chooses to preserve his life, does this decision have moral import. John Stuart Mill believes, on the contrary, that the man who by inclination promotes the general good is more virtuous than the man who promotes the general good against his natural inclination, since the actor's own happiness must be taken into account when weighing his virtue. According to Mill, increasing happiness is the sole object of virtue. Actions of a class which, if practiced generally, would work against the general good, are proscribed. The best proof of a good character, according to Mill, is good actions, not good will. Kant and Mill would undoubtedly agree on many practical issues requiring moral judgment, but where they disagree, rational argument would prove impossible. Each would deny the basic criteria by which the other defines the Good.

G. E. Moore's (1963) moral intuitionism, contained in his statement, "Good is good and that is the end of the matter," presupposes that all of us agree as to what is good in the same sense that we agree as to what is yellow; Moore sees our basic principles as self-justifying in that they are self-evident, that is, they are clearly and distinctly true. But if, as seems evident to me, there exist incompatible worldviews which are equally complex and differentiated, then universalist positions in ethics such as those of Moore or Kant cannot be justified on rational grounds.

Theories of Justification

By what criteria is it possible to justify one's choice of ultimate values? Theories of justification[1] are of three sorts: (1) obedience; (2) deontological; and (3) teleological.

Obedience

One may choose ultimate values by selecting a dogma based on revealed truths. Examples are Marxism, Christianity, or nationalism. Having accepted the dogma, one can then simply act in accord with the dictates of the party line. Justification by obedience—whether to God, country, or secular tradition—rejects the possibility of man being a morally autonomous agent. Man then becomes subordinate to the Creator of Truth, whether the creator is seen as God, Marx, or Nixon. In the words of Bishop Mortimer (1963):

> The first foundation is the doctrine of God the Creator. God made us and all the world. Because of that he has an absolute claim on our

[1] I am indebted to Frankena (1963) for his discussion of theories of justification.

obedience. We do not exist in our own right, but only as His creatures, who ought therefore to do and be what he desires. . . . "Of the fruit of the tree of the knowledge of good and evil thou shalt not eat" . . . .

From the doctrine of God as the Creator and source of all that is, it follows that a thing is not right simply because we think it is, still less because it seems to be expedient. It is right because God commands it [pp. 313–314].

The same Christian message is conveyed by Thomas Merton (1967):

It was the desire to "be as gods" . . . that led Adam and Eve to taste the fruit of the forbidden tree. . . . As long as we are on earth our vocation is precisely to be imperfect, incomplete, insufficient in ourselves, changing, hapless, destitute, and weak, hastening toward the grave [p. 105].

As an atheist, I reject obedience or faith as a basis for morality. In particular, I reject the premise that man should choose his ultimate values so that they accord with the revealed word of God. A Christian would say that I am guilty of the sin of pride. However, if one interprets "revealed word of God" as a metaphor for the nature of actual reality, then I would agree that man's highest spiritual aspirations must accord with his highest potential and be in harmony with the laws of his own nature and the external world.

Deontological

One may justify one's system of ultimate values by one or another deontological view, which is to say that the basic judgments of obligation are perceived as being given intuitively without recourse to consideration of what serves the common good. For deontologists such as Kant, the principle of justice or of truth or the value of life stands by itself without regard to any balance of good over evil for self, society, or the universe. For nontheistic deontologists, morality is, I suppose, equated with aesthetics, requiring of the moral individual a fine sensibility and intuition, and establishing in effect a moral individual a fine sensibility and intuition, and establishing in effect a moral elite. This is the view of Aristotle, when he states that the decision as to what determines the golden mean rests with perception. It is a view which detaches what man values from what is good for man, even in an ultimate sense. Since I believe that morality must serve man, and not man morality, I reject deontological systems of justification as well as those based on obedience.

Teleological

The last basis on which one may ground a system of values is teleological. The final appeal in a teleological system is nonmoral and is based on the comparative balance of good over evil to be produced in the end. Good may be defined hedonistically in terms of pleasure, or more loftily in terms of self-realization, perfection, or love. But in all instances, the good is defined as good for man. The theory of justification I accept is rule-teleology or rule-utilitarianism (sometimes also called ethical universalism); that is, that an act is right if and only if the *principle* under which it falls is thought to produce at least as great a balance of good over evil as any available alternative. Act-utilitarianism, by contrast with rule-utilitarianism, is concrete, presumptuous, tied to the present, and insufficiently elevating. It is *concrete*. A consistent act-utilitarian must calculate the morality of every situation anew without recourse to the guidance of overriding rules, an approach which leads to unavoidable and unresolvable difficulties. Act-utilitarianism, for example, would require of the individual that in each instance he calculate anew whether or not to obey the law against running a red light or stealing for personal gain. Rather than make these calculations, the non-principled actor will in many instances act opportunistically. This concrete approach to ethical judgement occurs in the individual at an early period of development and is usually superseded by appeal to rule and principle as soon as the individual is capable of abstract thought. Act-utilitarianism would seem, therefore, to restrict the moral sense to a rather primitive level. Act-utilitarianism is *presumptuous*. The actor presumes that he possesses insight superior to that of the distilled wisdom contained in the principle he disregards. Should a witness lie in a court of law to save a defendant he is sure is innocent? Joseph Fletcher (1966), the Situation Ethicist, answers: "Yes, he should lie if he believes the defendant would otherwise be found guilty." The deontologist answers: "No, a lie is always wrong." The rule-utilitarian answers: "No, if the court system is just, the common good is best served by truth-telling." Act-utilitarianism is *tied to the present*. Consider, for example, the guarantees of the rights of the accused or of the minority in the Bill of Rights. The exercise of these guarantees often creates a situation where the protection of the rights of an individual will not lead to a balance of good over evil for the majority of citizens. Act-utilitarians would therefore have to reject the Bill of Rights in these situations whereas rule-utilitarians would find these gaurantees consistent with their moral philosophy because the principle if made universal would benefit the common good. Act-utilitarianism is *insufficiently elevating*. Matters of conscience exercise different capacities and appeal to different motives in man than do matters of practical judgment. Suppose that act A and act B result in exactly the same ratio of cost to benefit, but act A involves deceit and breaking a contract, while act B involves purchasing a cocktail dress rather than a pair of badly needed walking shoes. A consistent act-utilitarian would view acts A and B as both equally wrong if they both produced an identical score on the minus side. But from the deontological viewpoint or that of rule-utilitarianism, act A must be regarded as more unethical than act B; otherwise, there is no moral but only a practical question to be decided.

The Good Life

So far we have discussed briefly alternative systems of moral judgment and theories of justification. At this point I want to present some of the principles of living which are consistent with attainment of what I view as the "Good Life." My definition of course is personal. Once accepted, however, it impels certain judgments concerning right and wrong conduct.

I view the Good Life as the life of self-realization and not the life of pleasure. The ordinary Western view, like that of the hedonists Epicurus and Bentham, is that pain is bad and to be avoided. But there is a tradition in philosophy that views suffering as good, not bad. With the existentialists, Aristotle, Nietzsche, the Hindu philosophers, and the Stoics, I believe that suffering is an important means by which man achieves the good, that is, self-mastery and knowledge of his higher nature. My position on this issue is more like that of the Hindus or Aristotle than like the Epicureans or Hedonists. That is, I regard self-chosen (but not inflicted) suffering as necessary for self-realization and therefore under certain circumstances as good. Since I regard the good life not as the pleasant or happy life but as the self-constructed, individuated, and self-examined life, it follows that I am more outraged by human acts which deprive others of their freedom of choice and their reason, than I am by human acts which create suffering. I am outraged by violations of the principle of informed consent in the research setting because this constitutes a justification of deceit and manipulation which in any situation deprives the participant of his freedom of rational choice.

The principle of justice (and its benevolent expression in the Golden Rule) is the keystone in my system of morality because the Good Life as I have defined it requires the balancing effects of justice to be achieved. The intrinsic worthwhileness of different kinds of good life may differ, and I may judge that the good I pursue is better than the good which someone else pursues. However, I am required by the principle of justice to grant that each person has an equal right to choose freely among known alternatives. Hence I interpret the Golden Rule to mean that I should grant to the other the same moral autonomy that I seek for myself. Thus there exists the moral necessity that an individual's consent be informed and freely given, except in those instances where the larger society judges the person not competent to be responsible for himself (e.g., the insane, the convicted criminal, the dependent minor). In such instances the concept of consent does not have meaning because free will entails responsibility for the consequences of freely chosen acts.

I place a high value on justice in all its meanings. *Retributive justice* rewards those who promote the good and punishes those who promote evil, thus increasing the occurrence of good through the Law of Effect. (My ethical system includes the relationship of enemy, i.e., of a relationship in which I desire the harm of another person. The ethics of revenge are a particular instance of the ethics of retributive justice and not relevant to this discussion, except that I can conceive of inflicting pain or insight upon another, but if I did so it would not be intended for his good or the Good.) *Commutative justice* requires the fulfillment of contractual obligations and means that a contractual agreement as to what constitutes the good of the parties concerned cannot be violated except by mutual consent. *Distributive justice* apportions privileges, duties, and responsibilities in accord with merit and recognizes that in any given situation individuals vary in what they can give and what they can receive, requiring from each in accord with his ability and giving to each in accord with his accomplishments.

My support of the rights of subjects is in the interests of justice, not mercy. Mercy implies that the giver is profferring a gift gratuitously, rather than that the recipient has a right to what he is given. Where justice appears to conflict with mercy, then justice should prevail. In such cases, when mercy is extended to one, there will necessarily be a violation of the rights of the community, and in the long run the result will be to promote evil. As development becomes more enlightened, these apparent conflicts are resolved by the understanding that justice is mercy and love is truth. However, even at less advanced stages of development, one must act, and to act means to accept the consequences of error seen retrospectively.

Function of Morality

What social and individual function does morality serve? Why should the research psychologist concern himself with the rights of subjects at all?

Concerning the social function, morality in man replaces the rule of instinct in other creatures, facilitating the survival of the species. The social motive to be moral comes from the same source as man's other motives—the urge to survive and flourish. Prudence or self-interest is the initial motive for all morality, and it remains the most dependable motive throughout life. Prudential reasons for an action are sufficient justification provided that they do not conflict with higher-level moral considerations. Wisdom refines and educates self-interest, leading to enlightened self-interest. Enlightened self-interest differs from narrow self-interest in that it recognizes reality constraints imposed by:

1. The future interest of the person himself
2. The dependence of the person upon his in-groups
3. The power of the larger community to reward and punish

Kant's dichotomy of the prudential and the moral does not seem defensible. Self-interest includes the moral; the moral includes the prudential. When we judge an act to be immoral we are really saying that in the long run the commission of acts of that sort would harm the larger community, and therefore in the long run harm the individual committing those acts. When we judge an act as immoral in most settings but not immoral in the research setting, or when we admit the act is immoral but do not censure it in the research setting, we are saying that there are extenuating circumstances in the research setting which do not exist in other settings. This is a dangerous justification for an action. Perhaps it is not the setting which is special but our relation to the setting. But each relation of an individual to a setting could be regarded as special and any exception as justified by the situation.

In addition to facilitating the survival of the species, morality serves the prudential, hedonistic, and spiritual motives of the individual man. Morality serves the prudential motive by guarding the long-range interests of the individual against momentary, shifting impulses. It serves the hedonistic motive by placing obstacles which magnify ultimate satisfaction. As Freud (1950) put it:

> It is easy to show that the value the mind sets on erotic needs instantly sinks as soon as satisfaction becomes readily obtainable. Some obstacle is necessary to swell the tide of the libido to its height; and at all periods of history, wherever natural barriers in the way of satisfaction have not sufficed, mankind has erected conventional ones in order to be able to enjoy love. . . . In this context it may be stated that the ascetic tendency of Christianity had the effect of raising the psychical value of love in a way that heathen antiquity could never achieve; it developed greatest significance in the lives of the ascetic monks, which were almost entirely occupied with struggles against libidinous temptation [p. 213].

Finally morality, like art, serves the spiritual motive in man by enhancing the meaning of the moment. It does so by endowing it with symbols and tying it to myth; thus man affirms his own higher nature.

CRITIQUE OF THE REVISED CODE OF ETHICAL STANDARDS OF PSYCHOLOGISTS

My specific criticism of the revised code of ethics are ground in the metaethical and ethical beliefs which I have just expressed.

The ethical problems we are about to consider are revealed clearly in this excerpt from the recently adopted Code of Ethics of the American Psychological Association (Committee on Ethical Standards in Psychological Research, 1973):

> There remains a serious and controversial issue to be noted. One frequently hears it asserted that behavioral research is contributing directly to the moral ills of society. According to this argument, when an investi-

gator invades the privacy of another person, employs deceit, or occasions pain or stress, he contributes to legitimizing these indignities, and therefore to their prevalence in interpersonal behavior. Many psychologists discount such claims, noting that it is quite easy for a research participant to understand the reasons for these behaviors when they occur in a research context and to distinguish them from their counterparts in everyday life. . . .

While we have no way of knowing whether behavioral research has in fact become an important causal factor in the current social malaise— the attrition of human relationships reflected in depersonalization and distrust with which many sensitive observers of the present-day human condition are concerned—we believe that psychologists would not accept the prospect that research in particular fields of psychology might become careless of human feelings and welfare [p. 17].

In my view, the worrisome issue to which the committee alludes in the above quote was not resolved by the revised Code of Ethics. I have two fundamental objections to the moral philosophy contained in that code.

Critique of the Ethical Stance Contained in the Revised Code

My first objection is that it *appeals to conventional rather than post conventional standards*. The committee stated in its 1972 version that its function was "to determine, crystallize, and make explicit" the "prevailing viewpoint among American psychologists regarding ethical standards for research" [Cook, Hicks, Kimble, McGuire, Schoggen, and Smith, 1972, p. 1]. It therefore polled its members to determine their thinking. But can the function of ethical philosophy, which is to improve clarity of thought and consistency of reasoning on ethical matters, be achieved by this method? I think not. From the time of Socrates most moral philosophers have stated categorically that moral principles cannot be defined by consensus, although the facts in a case can be judged by peer consensus. Customary or group morality is at a lower level of reasoning than rational or reflective morality. Reflective or post-conventional morality must be logically consistent with a system of tenets, while conventional morality need only reflect the prevailing view at a given time. In fact, there is no prevailing viewpoint among psychologists, but rather many viewpoints, diametrically opposed to each other in important ways. Thus the committee, if it performed its function as it defined that function, could not make a definitive statement of normative ethics. The present document admirably reflects the values and interests of all factions, but does so by violating certain fundamental tenets of each rather than by synthesizing their essential components. In contrast to situation ethics (Fletcher, 1966) which recognizes but one principle—that of love—the code recognizes 10 ethical principles. These are stated clearly and in meaningful detail, presumably so that the investigator will know whether or not he has violated an ethical principle. On the other hand, the investigator has few, if any, firm guidelines to determine whether or not it is *wrong* for him to violate an ethical principle. Indeed, he is provided by the code with many reasons why he can, and even should, violate any given principle.

My second objection to the ethical stance contained in the code *concerns the cost-benefit type of analysis for resolving ethical conflicts, which the committee adopted.* In my view, a cost-benefit approach to ethics desensitizes rather than elevates ethical sensibilities. According to the code, when a conflict between scientific rigor and the rights of subjects arises, the experimenter's ethical obligations to the subjects may be superseded. To be specific, the following rights of the subject are recognized explicitly but can be suspended in the interests of scientific rigor:

1. The right of the subject to be involved in research only with his knowledge and informed consent (principles 3 and 5)
2. The right of the subject to be dealt with in an open and honest manner (principles 4 and 8)
3. The right of the subject to protection from physical and mental distress and loss of self-esteem (principle 7)
4. The right of the subject to a clear and fair contractual agreement (principle 6)

Referring to the cost-benefit approach by which such violations are justified, the code states:

> Almost any psychological research with humans entails some choice of one particular ethical consideration over others. For this reason, there are those who would call a halt to the whole endeavor, or who would erect barriers that would exclude research on many central psychological questions. But for psychologists, the decision not to do

> research is in itself a matter of ethical concern since it is one of their obligations to use their research skills to extend knowledge for the sake of ultimate human betterment [Committee on Ethical Standards, 1973, p. 7].

In making this judgment, the investigator needs to take account of the potential benefits likely to flow from the research in conjunction with the possible costs, including those to the participants, that the procedures entail.

> An analysis following this approach asks about any procedure, "Is it worth it, considering what is required of the research participant and other social costs, on the one hand, and the importance of the research, on the other?" Or, "Do the net gains of doing the research outweigh the net gains of not doing it?" The decision may rule against doing the research, or it may affirm the investigator's positive obligation to proceed. Such an analysis is also useful in making choices between alternatives on potential gains from the research?" [Committee on Ethical Standards, 1973, p. 11.]

The cost-benefit analysis contained in the above quotes follows from the hedonic calculus of Jeremy Bentham, who was an act-utilitarian. The application of the hedonic calculus leads to subjective relativism and moral dilemmas. The revised code assumes moral dilemmas are inevitable in the research endeavor; but the function of a system of moral philosophy is precisely to avoid such dilemmas. A code of ethics for the American Psychological Association should set forth principles of obligation which guide all members in determining what is morally right, wrong, and obligatory, and which prohibit blatant violations of subjects' rights on the part of experimenters. Its function, in my opinion, is to state clearly the obligations of experimenters to subjects in such a form that differences which arise in a debate about what is good or right in the research setting can be resolved reliably and equitably. My objection to the approach taken by the committee in drafting the code (Cook, Kimble, Hicks, McGuire, Schoggen, & Smith, 1971; Cook et al., 1972) is simply that the function of a code of ethics, as I define it, could not be served. That is, the experimenter would not be morally obliged to bring his behavior into conformity with clearly stated principles of conduct. In point of fact, the use of a cost-benefit analysis serves to legitimate the loophole known as the "moral dilemma," that is, the situation in which the actor believes that he is forced to choose between *equally* culpable alternatives.

The cost-benefit analysis becomes particularly onerous when the individual or group calculating the ratio is an interested rather than a disinterested party. It is questionable whether a physician has the right to determine for a patient the balance of risk over benefit of alternative treatment plans; but it is certain that the physician is not morally privileged to pass judgment concerning the balance of risk to the patient against the benefit to mankind of using the patient as a guinea pig in a medical experiment. That decision to risk his personal welfare belongs entirely to the patient, and he must, without qualification, have access to all the information the doctor has about how that treatment may affect him in order that he (and not the physician) may make that decision knowledgeably. The investigator, by withholding information from the subject, in effect imposes his perspective concerning what is good for mankind on the subject, rather than leaving that choice to the subject.

In accord with rule-utilitarianism, an act is judged as right if, and only if, the rule under which it falls will, generally speaking, produce a balance of good over evil for man as a species. Where the good of the species and the good of the subgroup do not conflict, then the act should also maximize the good of the subgroup. Where the good of the species and the subgroup do not conflict with the good of the individual, then the act should maximize the good of the individual as well. It is the duty of a person to develop his moral sense to its highest possible level. At the highest level of development (seldom reached in practice) a person could reconcile the interests of his community, the subgroup of which he is a member, and his individual needs (both his higher and his lower inclinations). It is a man's duty insofar as possible to avoid provoking situations which create conflicts of obligation, since such conflicts by definition result in harm to some. Act-utilitarianism presented as a cost-benefit analysis readily lends itself to opportunistic interpretation, whereas rule-teleology or, for that matter, rule-deontology would not.

In addition to my moral objections to a cost-benefit analysis, the difficulties inherent in trying to calculate in quantitative terms the merits of a proposed program of research against the extent to which a subject's human rights have been violated, are insurmountable. It *is* possible, however, to determine whether the proposed violation accomplishes what the experimenter claims it would accomplish; e.g., whether by deceit, subject naivité is assured. It is also possible to determine whether a jury of the subject's peers would judge the proposed treatment to be harmful. If certain acts are not proscribed without qualification (as I think they should be) then, consistent with its act-utilitarian stance, the code should require an investigator who plans to violate the *basic* human rights of a subject to demonstrate:

1. To a committee of his peers that (a) his objectives if achieved would have scientific or social merit; (b) his experimental procedures which violate the rights of subjects are necessary to his objectives, and will in fact further these objectives significantly better than alternative methods which would not violate the rights of subjects; and (c) his debriefing procedures will in fact remove the undesirable consequences of his procedures.
2. To a committee of his prospective subjects' peers that (a) his objective if achieved would have social significance from their point of view; and (b) the indignities suffered by the subjects are not excessive in view of the social significance of the research, so that they would not be likely to lose confidence in the trustworthiness of behavioral scientists. Pilot subjects should agree, at the 5% level of confidence, that "there is sufficient reason for the concealment or misrepresentation that, on being fully informed later on . . . , the research participant [will] be expected to find it reasonable, and to suffer no loss of confidence in the integrity of the investigator or of others involved" [Committee on Ethical Standards, 1973, p. 37].

Issue of Informed Consent

We come now to the crucial issue of informed consent. Any moral system which values in man his reason and moral autonomy will allow few exceptions to the rule of informed consent. By moral autonomy is meant the right and obligation of each mature, healthy human being to assume personal responsibility for his actions. I would regard the right of the subject to choose freely to participate in research as inviolable, not to be abridged by the investigator, although it may be waived by the subject. In my view, doing research on people without their knowledge and informed consent is unethical under all circumstances. Certainly if used as a subject without his knowledge or consent, the subject must be fully informed after the fact about what was actually going on. Principle 3 of the code reads:

> Ethical practice requires the investigator to inform the participant of all features of the research that reasonably might be expected to influence willingness to participate, and to explain all other aspects of the research about which the participant inquires. [But then the qualification:] Failure to make full disclosure gives added emphasis to the investigator's responsibility to protect the welfare and dignity of the research participant [Committee on Ethical Standards, 1973 p. 29].

Principle 5 reads:

> Ethical research practice requires the investigator to respect the individual's freedom to decline to participate in research or to discontinue participation at any time. The obligation to protect this freedom requires special vigilance when the investigator is in a position of power over the participant. [But then the qualification:] The decision to limit this freedom increases the investigator's responsibility to protect the participant's dignity and welfare [Committee on Ethical Standards, 1974, p. 42].

Contained within each of these principles is a qualification which permits the principle to be violated. The qualifications are discussed in some detail in the body of the document. These qualifications indirectly apply to principle 6 as well, which reads:

> Ethically acceptable research begins with the establishment of a clear and fair agreement between the investigator and the research participant that clarifies the responsibilities of each. The investigator has the obligation to honor all promises and commitments included in that agreement [Committee on Ethical Standards, 1973, p. 54].

A subject who has been deceived as to the nature of his agreement cannot enter into a clear and fair agreement in the first place. These qualifications are not wrong because the subject may be exposed to suffering, but because a subject deprived of the right to informed consent has been deprived of his ability to decide freely and rationally how he wishes to dispose of his time and person. An experimenter should not ask subjects to risk pain, deception, or embarrassment unnecessarily or for trivial reasons or without just recompense. But if the subject has been informed fully as to the circumstances and possible risk to his person, dignity, and self-esteem, then no important ethical principle has been violated even if he consents to undertake considerable risk.

The right of subjects to informed consent has been burlesqued by at least one recent experiment, to demonstrate no doubt that psychology would suffer if that right were guaranteed. The experiment I have in mind was reported in the February 1973 issue of the *American Psychologist* (Resnick & Schwartz, 1973). The investigators sought to determine the effect of complying with the revised code by contrasting the responses of subjects who were presented with a verbal conditioning task in the usual way, and subjects who were presented with the task in a way which they thought was required by principles 3, 4, and 5 of the new ethics code. The investigators interpreted these standards to mean that they must fully brief the subject and that their briefing must include a lengthy explanation of the alternative hypotheses of the experimenters. The experimenters informed the subject as to how he would be expected to behave if he did permit himself to be verbally conditioned, and explained to the subject that they wished to determine the effects of full disclosure of the hypotheses on each subject's behavior in order to help resolve a recent controversy among psychologists concerning the ethical standards by which such research should be conducted. Needless to say, these rather ridiculous experimental instructions resulted in fewer instances of verbal conditioning than the standard instructions. In many instances the subjects reacted negativistically, a finding which would be predicted by Brehm's (1966) theory of psychological reactance. This experiment does not test the actual effects of compliance with the new code on psychological research, except in those few instances in which experimenters behave in an absurdly pedantic and self-destructive way; the code certainly does not require that they do so. The experiment burlesques the meaning of informed consent, since there was nothing unethical in the original instructions or the so-called unethical condition. In that condition, subjects were merely not informed of the experimenters' hypotheses that reinforced pronouns would show a greater frequency. The experimenter's hypothesis about how the subject will behave is his own business and the principle of informed consent does not require that the experimenter share his hypotheses with his subjects. The ethical experimenter should explain to curious prospective subjects that complete disclosure of the investigator's hypotheses might affect their responses and that therefore these hypotheses cannot be shared until all subjects have been seen. Provided that the experimenter keeps his promise to share his hypotheses and that subjects who object to delayed feedback have the opportunity to refuse to participate, the right of informed consent is in no way abridged.

It is true, however, that university committees entrusted by HEW with the protection of human subjects are interpreting their duties in an overzealous way which is unduly restrictive of the activities of investigators, perhaps in order to protect the university itself from risk. Thus, at the University of California at Berkeley, the same ethics committee which formulated an outstanding statement concerning the rights of subjects and the obligations of experimenters devised an obligatory consent form which many researchers, with good reason, find objectionable. While the investigator should be required to discuss possible risks and benefits to the subject and to take full responsibility for minimizing the former and maximizing the latter, he should certainly not be required to suggest to subjects that harm is likely to come to them as a result of participating in the proposed study. Neither should the subject be required to sign a form stating that he understands and implicitly accepts the specified risks and benefits. The subject deserves a full disclosure of the relevant aspects of the research which might affect his decision to participate. Only he can define which aspects entail risks and which benefits to himself. It is as presumptuous as it is embarrassing for an investigator to place labels on his subject's experience prior to its occurrence.

Issue of Experimental Deception and Manipulation

A second critical issue in the application of normative ethics to the research experience concerns the use of experimental deception and manipulation of the subject.

The Moral Problem

There is no ethical system, as far as I know, which condones deceit, lie telling, and the breaking of contracts. Not even the ethical egoism of Epicurus and Nietzsche, which holds that one should always do what promotes one's own greatest good, condones such practices, since there is substantial empirical reason to doubt that one's own good is in the long run served by deceiving others. Experimental deception is not a well-kept secret, and in fact has invited deception in return. If egoistic theories of ethics do not justify deception, neither does the rule-utilitarianism of John Stuart Mill. The rule proscribing deceit, lie telling, and contract breaking is viewed as conducive to the common good. The relativist positions of both the hedonists and the utilitarians, as well as all universalist positions of ethics, theological and secular, seem to agree that a man should not lie for gain nor deceive his neighbor into agreeing to an unfair contract.

Telling the truth and keeping promises are regarded as obligatory in most systems of ethics for many compelling reasons. Perhaps the most compelling of all is that belief in the coherence of the universe cannot be maintained without contract. Contracts and promises provide the same security in the social world which invariant cause-and-effect relations provide in the physical world. Without invariant cause-and-effect relations in the physical universe, goal-oriented behavior would be impossible. Imagine a situation in which turning a doorknob could release a stream of lemonade or trigger a gun or any number of other possibilities, as well as open a door. Only by acting in accord with agreed-upon rules, keeping promises, and avoiding deceit can human beings construct for themselves a coherent, consistent environment in which purposive behavior becomes possible.

It is part of the human condition that man seeks a system of central beliefs and values to elevate, integrate, and illuminate the purposive strivings of everyday life. In epochs where faith prevails, man is able to externalize the source of his system of tenets. He projects and reifies his need to find meaning in relationships with work or other persons, and "believes in" God, or progress, or communism, or science, or country. Ours is not an epoch where faith prevails. The ideas of science, progress, communism, country, and God do not inspire belief as they once did. But those of us who are unbelievers in an omnipotent, omniscient, and loving Deity also require lawfulness and coherence in the universe. Without rules against deceit and manipulation, the construction of a consistent environment to facilitate effective functioning would be impossible.

The effects upon subjects which I judge to be most harmful are those which result in cynicism, anomie, and hopelessness. In my view, the worst thing that can happen to a person is for him to lose faith in the possibility of constructing for himself a meaningful life. Any experience which diminishes that faith inflicts suffering and possible

Metaethical and Normative Considerations

harm. College students, who are the most frequently used subject pool, are particularly susceptible to conditions that produce an experience of anomie. My former secretary, Paula Lozar, who is also a doctoral candidate in English literature and was born into the Catholic faith, when typing an earlier version of this paper described an incident which illustrates the way in which deception in an experimental setting can contribute to the feeling of anomie in young people. Not only does it illustrate sensitivity to loss of faith in the meaningfulness of life, but also the heightening of this sensitivity by an upbringing emphasizing Catholic notions of merit and the sinfulness of pride in one's accomplishments. Lozar (personal communication, 1971) writes about the incident, which she remembers vividly although it occurred 10 years ago, as follows:

> When I was 18, a sophomore in college a psychologist from a nearby clinic came to my dormitory one evening and explained that he was looking for subjects for an experiment which involved simply telling stories about pictures which would be shown them. This sounded interesting, so I signed up. At the interview the same psychologist introduced me to a girl a few years my senior, who stayed bland and noncommittal throughout the time she interviewed me. She showed me a few pictures, and since they were extremely uninteresting I felt that the stories I was making up must be very poor. But she stopped at that point and told me that I was doing very well. I was gratified and said something to that effect before we went on to the rest of the pictures. Then I filled out a form about my reactions to the interview, and experimenter, etc., and she took it and left. After being alone for a few minutes, I looked around the office and noticed a list of the last names of subjects, with "favorable" and "unfavorable" written alternately after each one. Shortly thereafter the male psychologist returned and said that, as I had guessed, what the interviewer had said had nothing to do with my performance. They were testing the effects of praise and dispraise on creative production, and he said so far they had discovered that dispraise had negative effects and praise seemed to have none at all. Since I expressed interest, he promised that the subjects would be given full results when they were tabulated. (But we never heard from him.)
>
> My reaction to the experiment at the time was mixed. I assumed that the deception was necessary to get the proper reaction from me, and that since I had behaved unsuspiciously the results of the experiment were valid. However, I was embarrassed at having been manipulated into feeling pride at a non-achievement and gratification at praise I didn't deserve. Nevertheless, I felt that it was "right" that I was embarrassed, since I had always been taught a "pride goeth before a fall' philosophy of achievement. Since in my early years in school I had alternated be-

tween being praised for doing well and being damned for doing *too* well, I had always been a poor judge of my own achievements and had no internal standards for evaluating my performance—although I knew I was very intelligent and felt that some sort of moral flaw kept me from doing as well as I might. At the time, I was attending a second-rate college and felt (rightly) that my grades had nothing to do with how well I was really doing relative to my ability. This experiment confirmed my conviction that standards were completely arbitrary. Furthermore, for several years I had followed a pattern of achievement which it took me another five years to get free of: I would go along for quite a while doing well in classes, interpersonal relations, etc. Then I would have a moment of hubris in which I was more self-confident or egotistical than it behooved me to be in that situation. At this point someone would cut me down to size; I would be totally devastated, and it would take me a long time to work myself up to my previous level of performance. The experiment had, in a lesser degree, the same effect upon me, and it may have served to confirm me in this pattern because the devastating blow was struck by a psychologist, whose competence to judge behavior I had never doubted before [Baumrind, 1971].

At a symposium on the ethics of research at the April 1972 meeting of the Western Psychological Association, one of the participants, Dr. Dawes (1972), read the above account to the audience and commented:

I suspect that if a member of another species were studying the psychology of the human race, he might find our ethical concerns confusing, if not downright weird. We seem to be concerned about incredibly subtle effects and unconcerned about much more blantant ones. Why [p. 7]?

In response to his comments, Lozar (personal communication, 1972) replied:

Dr. Dawes raises two questions which I would like to answer—first he questions the "implicit belief" that a single experiment could have such a "catastrophic effect" as I described; and second, he characterizes this "catastrophic effect" as so "incredibly subtle" that only a "weird" researcher could possibly be concerned about it. It is not a matter of "belief" but of fact that I found the experience devastating. I told literally *no one* about it for eight years because of a vague feeling of shame over having let myself be tricked and duped. It was only when I realized that I was not peculiar but had, on the contrary, had a *typical* experience that I first recounted it publicly. . . .
At the time of the experiment I had arrived at a position *common* to young adults who have lost confidence in external standards, either

ideals or authorities, as a guide to how to live, and was in the process of formulating my own standards. As a result of my early lack of self-confidence and inconsistent school experiences, my task had been laborious and not entirely successful, as the account Dr. Dawes read to you indicated. The experiment confirmed me in my lack of success. I had been led into a situation where I was explicitly told to disregard my own interpretation of what was going on and made to perceive it another way, and then eventually told that *both* ways I had perceived it were wrong. . . . The result was to further convince me that my perceptions were useless as a guide for action, and that, since the only person I felt I could trust—myself—was not trustworthy, I had no way of judging how to act and hence it was better not to act at all.. . .

I was harmed in an area of my thinking which was central to my personal development at that time. To me, and to most of my classmates, the task of setting one's own standards, of formulating guides to living, was more than an "incredibly subtle" peripheral concern; it was one of the most important tasks we faced. This had, incidentally, nothing to do with a conviction of the "meaningfulness" of life, but rather with one's ability to *give* meaning to one's own life. I rather suspect that many of us who volunteered for the experiment were hoping to learn something about ourselves that would help us to gauge our own strengths and weaknesses, and formulate rules for living that took them into account. Something of the sort was, I know, in the back of my own mind. When, instead, I learned that I did not have any trustworthy way of knowing myself—or anything else—and hence could I have no confidence in any life style I formed on the basis of my knowledge, I was not only disappointed, but felt that I had somehow been cheated into learning, not what I needed to learn, but something which stymied my very efforts to learn [Baumrind, 1972a, pp. 13–14].

The Methodological Problem

It is unlikely that any investigator would attempt to justify the use of deception on moral grounds without recourse to a cost-benefit analysis. The argument for the use of deception on the basis of such an analysis is contained in the following quotations from the Code of Ethics:

> The obligation to advance the understanding of significant aspects of human experience and behavior is especially likely to impinge upon well-recognized human rights. Significant research is likely to deal with variables and methods that touch upon sensitive human concerns. And if ambiguity in causal inference is to be reduced to a minimum—an essential of good science—research must be designed in ways that, on occasion, may make the relationship between the psychologist and the human research participant fall short of commonly held ideals for human relationships. . . .

> Not only do ethical questions follow from the psychologist's pursuit of important independent and dependent variables but the methods that are adequate to make inferences as unambiguous as possible tend to be the ones that raise ethical difficulties. Many psychologists believe (though some question this) that to obtain valid and generalizable data, it is often essential that the research participants be naive. The requirements of research may thus seem to demand that the participants be unaware of the fact that they are being studied, or unaware of what is being studied or of the hypothesis under investigation. Or deception may appear to be necessary if a psychological reality is to be created under experimental conditions that permit valid inference [Committee on Ethical Standards, 1973, pp. 8–9].

Contained in these quotes is the basic rationale for the experimental method, a rationale which many scientists are calling into question (e.g., Chein, 1972; Guttentag, 1971; Harré & Secord, 1972; Kelman, 1966; and Orne, 1972). Schultz (1969), for example, concludes in his critical examination of the history of human experimentation:

> It is suggested that psychology's image of the human subject as a stimulus-response machine is inadequate and that many studies are based on data supplied by subjects who are neither randomly selected nor assigned, nor representative of the general population, nor naïve, and who are suspicious and distrustful of psychological research and researchers [p. 214].

Brandt (1971) states:

> Psychological experiments with human subjects are frequently based on faulty assumptions which may lead not only to erroneous conclusions but also to warped ethics. Motivational studies often assume implicitly and without empirical evidence different motives in E and in S for participating in the experiment. The principle of parsimony requires a single explanation for E's and S's behavior, when it is virtually identical. Milgram's experiments on "obedience" . . . illustrate the application of identical explanatory principles to E's and S's behavior and are shown to have tested the release of aggression in a situation which facilitated the use of rationalization and displacement. Experiments with human S's are shown to be undemocratic and unnecessary in instances where the behavior of the S's can be predicted from E's behavior [p. 231].

According to Brandt's analysis, both Milgram (1963) and his subjects were enabled to release aggression because each had recourse to the same convenient rationalization—the aggression was justified by the scientific value of the end. The construct "destructive obedience" was as spurious a description of the motivation of the subjects as it would have been of the experimenter's motivation.

Holland (1968), focusing his analysis on the deception manipulation, demonstrated with three experiments that a high percentage of Milgram's subjects probably detected the deception without Milgram's knowledge. Mixon (1972) argues, as I did in my critique of the Milgram experiments (Baumrind, 1964), that subjects may always be expected to suppose the existence of at least minimal precautions to safeguard their physical well-being, and that therefore the judgment that Milgram's obedient subjects behaved in a "shockingly immoral" fashion is quite gratuitous.

Other investigators challenge the belief that subjects are indeed naive. These investigators believe that many subjects role-play the naive subject. Wahl (1972) has summarized the growing body of evidence that deception in psychological research is not effective and subjects are not naive. He documents his assertion that the assurance of subject naiveté by deception is neither theoretically nor practically defensible, and that experimental realism is not necessarily achieved better by situations using deception than by situations not using deception. Moreover, Wahl concludes from his review that experimenters cannot distinguish subjects for whom the deception promotes experimental realism from subjects who merely pretend to be fooled. If the widespread use of deceit has decreased the likelihood that subjects will be naive, as Wahl's survey suggests, such practices are obviously counterproductive. If the sample to be used in any given study is biased already (such as jaded lower-division psychology students), then the argument that informed consent may be dispensed with in order to assure an unbiased sample becomes unconvincing. The *assumption* that ambiguity in causal inference is in fact reduced to a minimum by procedures that deceive and manipulate subjects has not been proven.

Guttentag (1971), in her critical examination of the experimental paradigm, questions the main distinction which is generally drawn between observational and experimental data; i.e., that it is possible to draw inferences from the latter but not from the former:

> Although the classical model holds sway in psychology, there are a number of issues which continue to be raised about it and the logic of statistical inference with which it is associated....
>
> The independence of the subject and experimenter is difficult to

assume in much research, especially evaluation research. Each observation of behavior, and each record of data is inevitably subjective. . . . Another problem is the experimenter's assumption of an essential independence and neutrality of each subject unit; i.e., that human beings are interchangeable. . . . Although the logic of experimentation and of statistical inference requires the assumption, one may still question whether it is a tenable one. . . .

Even when the individuals from such populations are randomly assigned to experimental conditions; given that people live within social systems, there is no logical guarantee that some condition which affects all subjects uniformly, a condition unknown to the experimenter, is not interacting with the experimental variables to produce a particular set of findings [pp. 80–81].

Given cogent critiques such as these of the assumption that ambiguity in causal inference can be reduced substantially by the use of deception, it seems difficult to defend the practice, even from a cost/benefit approach to ethics.

Yet the use of deception and manipulation continues to be the rule rather than the exception. From my experience in the last year of talking to university audiences on matters of ethics, I have learned that deception and manipulation still characterize the research of graduate and undergraduate students in social psychology, and that indeed many students, with the blessings of their instructors, are much more concerned with designing a clever set of manipulations, than in designing an equally clever research plan which avoids the manipulation of subjects. It is my observation that investigators concerned about the effects of revealing deceptive practices are increasingly opting for leaving the subjects misinformed. I predict that unless the code contains an unequivocal proscription of this practice, its use will become widespread until subjects eventually become aware of the practice, thus negating its positive effects from the investigator's point of view.

An example which recently came to my attention is fairly typical, illustrating rather well how little attention is paid to ethical issues by instructors in charge of training undergraduate and graduate students. A competent undergraduate at one of the smaller but highly respected campuses of the University of California wished to study nonverbal communication. She devised a gadget for recording instances of the behavior which interested her; this gadget could be operated without the knowledge of the subject. She recruited student subjects on the pretext that she wished to interview them concerning their social and political attitudes. She never debriefed her subjects, and it should be noted that her faculty sponsor did not raise the ethical issue with her. During the course of her study several friends questioned the ethics of her procedures, which led her to wonder how her subjects would feel if they discovered that they had been duped. Now concerned about the effects of her deceitful instructions, the student-experimenter decided to actually analyze her interview data as a way of sparing her subjects the knowledge that they had been deceived. The student, like other more mature investigators, felt that the real harm would come from the debriefing itself. Was the scientific value of the study sufficient to justify the use of deceit and failure to debrief? Since the question was never raised, how could it be answered? The student herself was learning to regard the use of deception as normative, and covert observation as acceptable. The methodological requirements of her study did in fact necessitate concealment. But there were ethical ways in which the concealment could have been accomplished. For example:

1. Subjects could have been selected from among those who agreed to accept the instructions as given, with the understanding that they would receive a full explanation subsequent to the study.
2. Nonverbal cues could have been recorded in connection with an actual social survey. Debriefing would include acknowledgment that additional information had been collected. Consent after the fact would be obtained from all subjects who were retained.

Instead, there was no debriefing, and the deception was supposedly defused by analyzing the data collected incidentally. Act-teleology as contained in the cost-benefit analyses would say that the harm to the subjects was nonexistent if deceptive debriefing were used and that therefore the entire deception was justified. Rule-teleology would say "openness and honesty are essential characteristics of the relationship between investigator and research participant" and that "respect for the dignity of the individual human being allows no compromise of the principle of informed consent" [Committee on Ethical Standards, 1973, pp. 29–30].

In my view, the investigator should forego the opportunity to engage in research that permits only two possible alternatives: *deceptive debriefing* (in which the truth is withheld from the subject because full disclosure would lower the subject's self-esteem or affect the research adversely) or *inflicted insight* (in which the subject is given insight into his flaws, although such insight is painful to him and although he has not bargained for such insight). In section 8-9 concerning the obligation of the investigator to remove misconceptions about the subject himself or his performance in the experiment, whether these misconceptions have been deliberately or unintentionally induced, the question is asked but not answered: "Must the investigator correct misinformation even when this will be distressing to the participant?" [Committee on Ethical Standards, 1973, p. 76). The situation, as I see it, is this: the investigator, to further his own end (i.e., to do worthy research as efficiently and effectively as possible) contrives a predicament for himself where, as he sees it, he must choose between two equally unacceptable alternatives in his treatment of subjects—that is, deceptive debriefing or inflicted insight. The solution to this "dilemma" is simple. The investigator need only reject his original experimental design as unethical on the grounds that it allowed him only two alternatives, both morally unacceptable (i.e., that it placed him in a moral dilemma). He can then proceed to invent another and more ethically acceptable design. No experimental procedure that could be anticipated by the investigator to require deceptive debriefing in order to guard the subject's self-esteem or mental health ought to be considered, as it violates the fundamental rights of the subject to have misconceptions removed subsequent to the experiment and to receive honest (although not necessarily complete) feedback concerning the findings of the experiment. The investigator's duty is clear. Just as he may not intentionally design an experiment in which it is necessary to kill or maim the subject in order to facilitate effective and efficient research, so he may not design an experiment in which it is necessary to deceptively debrief a subject.

THE VALUE OF THE BEHAVIORAL SCIENCES

The objections to my position on the ethics of research which I find most disturbing are those from scientists who feel that my position represents an attack on the value of science itself and therefore on the meaningfulness of the scientific enterprise to which they and I have chosen to commit our professional lives. For example, Reynolds (1971) feels that my views reflect:

a profound lack of confidence in the potential for scientific knowledge related to social and human phenomena to be of any benefit to society, present or future. . . . It is sad that a committed, professional social scientist considers that the major product of her, and her colleagues, research activities is impotent and trivial. If such an attitude is dominant among the members of professional social science organizations, it seems unlikely that a very significant body of knowledge related to social and human phenomena will ever develop, [pp. 7-8].

That I regard the work of my colleagues or my own work as trivial is untrue. It is true, however, that I place an even higher value on the *activities* of behavioral scientists and the *values* inherent in scientific activity, than on the *products* of that activity. The disciplined exercise of intelligence in science or art is of value in itself and this value does not depend upon the betterment of the material aspects of life to which it rightfully leads. The good the scientist pursues—truth, rationality, respect for evidence, tolerance of difference—is of intrinsic worth. But if the rule which justifies scientific experimentation is "You shall know the truth and the truth shall set you free," then that rule applies also in the conduct of science. The pursuit of truth cannot be used to justify deceit.

The research psychologist has many privileges not possessed by other people with whom the subject deals, and these privileges are granted to him on the assumption that he will be responsible, trustworthy, and altruistic in the conduct of his professional life. The investigator bears a heavy responsibility for the effects his actions have upon those others with whom he comes in contact professionally. For children, subjects, and students, the psychologist may serve as a model. Since his influence is magnified by his status, his responsibility to behave morally is correspondingly greater. Fundamental moral principles of reciprocity and justice are violated when the research psychologist, using his position of trust, acts to deceive or degrade those whose extension of trust is granted on the basis of a contrary role expectation. It is unjust to use naive—i.e., trusting—subjects, and then exploit their naiveté. More than most citizens, the researcher is required to accept full responsibility for the unintended consequences of his intended acts.

A subtle, implicit social contract binds experimenter and subject, in addition to the explicit contractual agreement stated in principle 6. In accord with their implicit social contract, the experimenter assumes that the subject trusts him and will obey his instructions, and the subject assumes that the experimenter is both knowledgeable and trustworthy. In view of the special vulnerability, both personal and moral, which the subject assumes by suspending disbelief and extending trust, the experimenter should agree to abide by a code of professional ethics more, not less, stringent than his personal code. The code of ethics to which the research psychologist pledges his adherence does not, so far as the potential subject knows, contain a "buyer beware" clause, nor does it state explicitly that the accumulation of knowledge has top priority in the investigator's hierarchy of values. The injury done the subject when the psychologist violates the subject's trust is not limited to the pain and humiliation that are the immediate consequences of this violation. The more serious harmful consequences may be that the subject is taught he cannot trust those who by social contract are designated as trustwotrhy. Furthermore, he may need to trust these role models in order not to feel alienated from the society. In addition to the harm done the subject, there is the larger harm done to the community when moral rules are violated and the violations are justified by the end they are said to serve. The harm done the individual in the name of good is the most unjust and degrading harm of all. If subjects can be deceived in the name of science, by what principle is it wrong to conduct holy wars in the name of Christianity or democracy?

There is no strategy of research in the behavioral sciences which can eliminate the investigator's subjectivity in the sense of his involvement with the object of his inquiry. Whether experimental objectivity enhances the quality of research is itself open to dispute. Many current philosophers of science, such as Polanyi (1958) and von Bertalanffy (1959), reject positivism as containing an insufficient view of man as a passive and finished object, and of the scientist as a neutral inquirer into what is, rather than what can be. These philosophers of science affirm the importance of personal knowledge as a guide both to observation and interpretation, and claim that the elimination of personal participation in the process of gaining knowledge is neither possible nor desirable. Man, who is the object of inquiry, is seen as a purposive, motivated, moral being engaged in the effort of self-construction. Man as psychologist is seen as a purposive, motivated, moral being engaged in the effort to understand the psychological reality of those he studies, so that he can master those aspects of social reality which have the most meaning to him. The research endeavor is seen as a special activity through which the investigator transcends his subjective experience and differentiates the universal from the idiosyncratic aspects of his personal knowledge.

BIBLIOGRAPHY

Baumrind, D. Some thoughts on ethics of research: After reading Milgram's "Behavioral study of obedience." *American Psychologist,* 1964, **19** (6), 421–423.

Baumrind, D. Principles of ethical conduct in the treatment of subjects: Reaction to the draft report of the Committee on Ethical Standards in Psychological Research. *American Psychologist,* 1971, **26** (10) 887–896.

Baumrind, D. Normative and metaethical considerations. Unpublished manuscript prepared for Symposium on Ethical Issues in the Experimental Manipulation of Human Beings, Western Psychological Association, Portland, Oreg., April 27, 1972a.

Baumrind, D. Reactions to the May 1972 draft report of the ad hoc Committee on Ethical Standards in Psychological Research. *American Psychologist,* 1972b, **27** (11), 1083–1086.

Brandt, L. W. Science, fallacies, and ethics. *The Canadian Psychologist,* 1971, **12** (2), 421–423.

Brehm, J. W. *A theory of psychological reactance.* New York: Academic, 1966.

Chein, I. *The science of behavior and the image of man.* New York: Basic Books, 1972.

Committee on Ethical Standards in Psychological Research. *Ethical principles in the conduct of research with human participants.* Washington, D.C.: American Psychological Association, Inc., 1973.

Cook, S. W., Hicks, L. H., Kimble, G. A., McGuire, W. J., Schoggen, P. H., & Smith M. B. Ethical standards for research with human subjects. Published for review and discussion. *APA Monitor,* May 1972, **3** (5), I–XIX.

Cook, S. W., Kimble, G. A. Hicks, L. H., McGuire, W. J., Schoggen, P. H., & Smith, M. B. Ethical standards for psychological research: Proposed ethical principles submitted to the APA membership for criticism and modification (by the) ad hoc Committee on Ethical Standards in Psychological Research. *APA Monitor,* July 1971, **2** (7), 9–28.

Dawes, R. M. Doing evil to others vs. seducing others to do evil. Unpublished manuscript prepared for Symposium on Ethical Issues in the Experimental Manipulation of Human Beings, Western Psychological Association, Portland, Oreg., April 27, 1972.

Fletcher, J. *Situation ethics: The new morality.* Philadelphia: Westminster, 1966.

Frankena, W. *Ethics.* Englewood Cliffs, N. J.: Prentice-Hall, 1963.

Freud, S. *Collected Papers, Vol. 4.* London: Hogarth, 1950.

Guttentag, M. Models and methods in evaluation research. *Journal of the Theory of Social Behavior,* 1971, **1** (1), 75–95.

Harré, R. & Secord, P. *The explanation of social behavior.* Oxford: Backwell, 1972.

Holland, C. H. *Sources of variance in the experimental investigation of behavioral obedience.* (Doctoral dissertation, University of Connecticut), Ann Arbor, Mich.: University of Microfilms, 1968, No. 69-2146.

Kelman, H. C. Deception in social research. *TransAction,* 1966, **3**, 20–24.

Kohlberg, L. Unpublished scoring manual for moral dilemma stories. Available from the author, Harvard University, Graduate School of Education, Laboratory of Human Development, Roy E. Larsen Hall, Appian Way, Cambridge, Mass 02138. 1971

Merton, T. *No man is an island.* New York: Image Books, 1967.

Milgram, S. Behavioral study of obedience. *Journal of Abnormal Social Psychology,* 1963, **67**, 371–378.

Mixon, D. Instead of deception. *Journal of the Theory of Social Behavior,* 1972, **2** (2), 145–177.

Moore, G. E. The subject matter of ethics. In R. Abelson (Ed.), *Ethics and metaethics: Readings in ethical philosophy.* New York: St. Martin, 1963.

Mortimer, R. C. The Bible and ethics. In R. Abelson (Ed.), *Ethics and metaethics: Readings in ethical philosophy.* New York: St. Martin, 1963.

Orne, M. T. On the social psychology of the psychological experiment: With particular reference to demand characteristics and their implications. *American Psychologist,* 1962, **17**, 776–783.

Polanyi, M. *Personal knowledge: Towards a post-critical philosophy.* Chicago: University of Chicago Press, 1958.

Resnick, J. H., & Schwartz, T. Ethical standards as an independent variable in psychological research. *American Psychologist,* 1973 **28** (2), 134–139.

Reynolds, P. Comments on "Principles of ethical conduct in the treatment of subjects: Reaction to the draft report of the Commitee on Ethical Standards in Psychological Research," by Diana Baumrind. Unpublished manuscript, September 1971.

Schultz, D. P. The human subject in psychological research. *Psychological Bulletin,* 1969, **72** (3), 214–228.

von Bertalanffy, L. Human values in a changing world. In A. Maslow (Ed.), *New knowledge in human values.* Chicago: Regnery, 1959.

Wahl, J. The utility of deception: An empirical analysis. Unpublished manuscript prepared for Symposium on Ethical Issues in the Experimental Manipulation of Human Beings, Western Psychological Association, Portland, Oreg., April 27, 1972.

CHAPTER 4

Ethical Issues in Research Involving Human Subjects*

Ernest Wallwork
Yale University
New Haven

When Professor Kennedy invited me to participate in this symposium, he suggested that I might use the occasion of responding to other speakers as an opportunity to develop my own ethical analysis of the American Psychological Association standards for research with human subjects. To do this, I must severely limit my critique of the other papers. Because Dr. Baumrind has identified several truly fundamental issues, I shall concentrate exclusively on the ethical assumptions in her paper that require further analysis. On the basis of a critique of Dr. Baumrind's philosophical position, I shall sketch an alternative ethical perspective on the APA code. This alternative perspective is closer to Professor McCormick's ethical theory than to

---

* In this paper, Dr. Wallwork was reacting to a version of Dr. Baumrind's paper that was earlier and less clearly formulated than the one in the preceding chapter.

the relativist assumptions shared by Drs. Baumrind and Smith, although it agrees with the general conclusions of the first two speakers.

Dr. Baumrind rightly attempts to clarify metaethical issues, for it is only on this basis that we can evaluate the new ethical standards for research with human subjects. Unfortunately, she has not succeeded in avoiding several major inconsistencies in justifying her conclusions. Consequently, several of her eminently worthy proposals about informed consent, committees, and the like are not supported by sufficiently impelling rational arguments and, hence, lack the persuasiveness they deserve. Dr. Smith implicitly recognizes this failure in rational persuasion when he dismisses Dr. Baumrind's ethical philosophy as a personal statement which has no stronger claim to validity than any other ethical position within the APA membership.

The first inconsistency in Dr. Baumrind's paper concerns the central issue of whether ethical disagreements, such as those over the APA code, are, in principle, capable of being resolved. At the outset of her paper, Dr. Baumrind flirts with an affirmative answer to this crucial issue in her statement that "most [ethical] differences are resolvable, at least in theory, provided that both participants have given some thought to normative and metaethical considerations and are prepared to debate the matter logically and in good faith." This statement apparently assumes that men share modes of ethical reflection as well as abstract principles that are sufficiently similar as to enable them to resolve most ethical disputes. This assumption regarding the resolvability of moral disputes similarly dominates her discussion of rule-utilitarianism as well as her critique of the new APA code.

Yet, Dr. Baumrind undermines this nonrelativist stance by arguing that ethical disagreements derive partly from incompatible worldviews containing fundamentally different values. For example, differences between Christians and Buddhists on the worth of human life are cited in support of the claim that these differences cannot be rationally resolved, although the example does not really prove, as Karl Dunker pointed out years ago, that an unresolvable moral disagreement really underlies this apparent conflict between Christians and Buddhists (Dunker, 1939; Wallwork, 1972, pp. 65–67). The differences separating members of the two faiths may result from different factual rather than moral evaluations, or they may be resolvable at higher levels of reasoning. Further developing this relativist position, Dr. Baumrind argues not only that men possess radically diverse views on "good and evil, right and wrong," but that they employ very different procedures of justification. In discussing Kant and Mill, for instance, Dr. Baumrind clearly states the thoroughgoing relativist thesis that "where they disagree, rational argument would prove impossible." This is a stronger claim than the supposition that we possess different values, for it suggests that we may find ourselves totally unable—like Kant and Mill—to resolve moral conflicts.

These conclusions about the impossibility of resolving moral disagreements are neither insignificant nor uninteresting. Dr. Baumrind is informing us that two conflicting ethical judgments are equally valid, there being no rational method of resolving moral conflicts. This undermines the validity of her entire argument, however, since her paper is obviously aimed at convincing us that her rule-teleology is superior to the ethical code formulated by the Ad Hoc Committee. Dr. Baumrind seems driven by the logic of her second line of reasoning to the unsatisfactory emotivist position that ethical claims are merely reflections of subjective desires, as expressed in the form "I approve of x, do so as well." If ethical judgments are merely emotional ejaculations, however, what is the point of rationally discussing the superiority of rule- over act-utilitarianism? Why bother discussing *reasons* for and against the ethical standards in the APA code?

In the final analysis, I do not believe Dr. Baumrind wishes to follow this route into emotivism and subjectivism, although crucial statements throughout her paper beg the real issues in favor of what I call "justification by personal reference"—as examplified by sentences beginning with "I believe," "As an atheist I reject," and so on. Evidence that she does not wish to follow this subjectivist route is suggested by her vague allusions to some sort of cognitive developmental theory which shows rule-utilitarianism to be more advanced and, therefore, cognitively adequate than act-utilitarianism. In this context, she speaks of being "logically and morally obligated" to adopt rule-utilitarianism. Unfortunately, the nature of this developmental theory is nowhere specified. If she were to accept Kohlberg's cross-cultural evidence for an invariant stage sequence of moral development, Dr. Baumrind would have to drop or at least clarify many of her relativist assumptions. For Kohlberg's research explicitly demonstrates that the disagreements she cites between philosophers, like Kant and Mill, and between religious cultures, like Christianity and Buddhism, are theoretically resolvable at the highest stage of moral reasoning, stage 6 (Kohlberg, 1971, pp. 163–180).

A second major inconsistency occurs in Dr. Baumrind's attempt to justify rule-utilitarianism in the absence of metaethical supports which provide the only possible rational defense of this position. Dr. Baumrind rests her argument for rule-utilitarianism on a critique of act-utilitarianism, but this leaves rule-utilitarianism as a purely formal, contentless, procedural process. As a process, rule-utilitarianism cannot itself establish the validity of the ends sought. Realizing this, Dr. Baumrind discusses the goals of rule-utilitarianism separately under the rubric, "the Good Life." These goals, focusing on self-realization, are nowhere justified, presumably because Dr. Baumrind does not possess a metaethical theory with which to rationally defend her ultimate value, self-realization. We are thus left with purely subjective goals on the one hand and a request that we apply rule-utilitarian calculations to advance them. Given the absence of compelling rational support for this position, I do not see how Dr. Baumrind can hope to gain our rational commitment to her personal values.

We might all agree that rule-utilitarianism is superior to act-utilitarianism, but differ on the goals or values to be advanced by the rules. Psychologists differing with Dr. Baumrind's goals might well substitute others—like the intrinsic value of knowledge (especially scientific knowledge of human behavior), the general welfare goal made possible by increased psychological insight, and the end of alleviating human ills through the application of psychological knowledge. Rules based on these alternative ends would not necessarily protect the individual rights with which Dr. Baumrind, with other morally sensitive individuals, is concerned.

Because Dr. Baumrind does not provide a sufficient ethical foundation for evaluating the new APA code, I would now like to sketch a more adequate way of ethically interpreting and criticizing it. In doing so, I will attempt to provide stronger support for some of Dr. Baumrind's conclusions regarding informed consent, deception, and the like. I feel it is incumbent upon me to do this, as I believe psychologists are rationally compelled to formulate stronger ethical standards for research involving human subjects and to monitor these principles more rigorously.

The new APA code is not, Dr. Baumrind's interpretation to the contrary, a form of act-utilitarianism, although I agree with her that it leaves the door open for rationalizations based upon act-utilitarian calculations. The reason the code is not a form of act-utilitarianism is found in the principles that modify strict cost-benefit analysis. While the Ad Hoc Committee has failed to indicate precisely how their cost-benefit recommendations relate to the code's principles, rules respecting informed consent, promise keeping, confidentiality, and so forth, are *always* to be taken into consideration in deciding upon the ethical acceptability of research. For example, if two studies have identical cost-benefit consequences, that study is to be preferred which has the higher degree of informed consent, the least deception, and the like. Or, to take a more likely example, if identical results can be obtained by two different procedures, the one that best conforms to the principles in the code is ethically preferable. The importance of rules, as well as cost-benefit calculations, is indicated by the committee's statement: "The nearest that the principles in this document come to an immutable 'thou shalt' or 'thou shalt not' is in the insistence that the human participant emerge from his research experience unharmed— or at least that he is exposed only to minimal risks to which he himself knowingly and freely consents—and, if possible, with an identifiable benefit" (Draft, May 1972, p. 2). The Ad Hoc Committee's detailed discussion of the code clearly indicates that act-utilitarian calculations based solely on cost-benefit analysis are qualified by the principles.

The mode of ethical reasoning used by the Ad Hoc Committee is best described by the features that characterize the fifth of Lawrence Kohlberg's six stages of moral development. Because Kohlberg's developmental theory is also a theory of increasing ethical adequacy, we may legitimately criticize the code from the next and highest level of moral reasoning, stage 6. It is noteworthy that this use of Kohlberg's theory to assess the code depends not upon the empirical validity of his developmental theory, but upon the logical superiority of stage 6 moral reasoning to stage 5.

The code expresses the following characterisitcs of the fifth stage, which follows the obedient orientation to fixed rules found at the preceding conventional stage. Stage 5 moralists believe rules should be established on a social-contract basis, involving democratic group discussion and agreement, such as that involved in formulating the APA code. Procedural rules for reaching consensus are stressed at this stage, because of clear awareness of the relativity of personal values and opinions. Aside from what is constitutionally and democratically agreed upon by a group, individual morality is seen as a matter of personal values and opinion, as the Ad Hoc Committee continually stresses in its discussion. Justice at this stage is seen primarily in terms of liberty, especially freedom of contract, rather than in terms of the substantive rights recognized at stage 6. In addition to emphasizing democratic constitutional procedures, this stage is also social utilitarian. Group rules are established with an eye to their utilitarian benefits. Outside these rules, free agreement and contract among individuals, such as that between a researcher and his informed subjects, is the principle means of establishing moral obligation (Kohlberg, 1971, pp. 199–204). The only way in which the Ad Hoc Committee departs from this otherwise apt description of their achievement is in formulating principles more ambiguously than one usually finds among stage 5 subjects. And this is obviously a major weakness in the code as Dr. Baumrind and other critics have rightly noted. Ideally, on stage 5 moral grounds, rules should act as a counterveiling force against the tendency of individuals to disregard them on the basis of special interests.

One basic problem with stage 5 moral reasoning which relates to the new code is its failure to justify an independent ethical stance against group rules that sanction or permit the violation of fundamental human rights. A second basic problem is that of moral consistency when different groups establish varying rules for identical cases. An example of the latter difficulty may be found among professional standards for research with human subjects. The fact that the codes of the medical, dental, sociological, and psychological professions are established on democratic constitutional grounds with an eye to utilitarian benefits does not prevent them from protecting (and neglecting) subjects differently as a result of varying goals and diverse professional interests. When conflicts between group rules and fundamental rights as well as among diverse group rules arise, morally sensitive men feel compelled to move beyond the confines of the formal contractual and rule-utilitarian orientations of stage 5. A new foundation for ethics is necessary in order to make this move, but, unfortunately, most men fail to find it.

This foundation is provided by a fresh, postrelativist atttempt to discover a universal morality on which all men could, in principle, agree. A morality on which universal agreement could be based requires that every rational moral agent could decide upon it whatever his circumstances, a criteria sometimes referred to as "the principle of reversibility" because it requires the agent to reverse role-taking with all parties in arriving at an acceptable decision (Kohlberg, 1971, pp. 204–213; Rawls, 1971). Two substantive moral principles derive from this search for universalizability. The first principle is that *"persons are of unconditional value,"* and are to be treated as ends, not as means (Kohlberg, 1971, p. 210). The second principle is *the right to equal justice*, or, "the right of every person to an *equal* consideration of his *claims* in every situation, not just those codified into law" or professional rules (Kohlberg, 1971, p. 210). These substantive rules are universalizable because every rational moral agent, as a matter of reflective policy, could agree that in similar situations each is to be respected and to be accorded the claims of equal justice. These principles are substantive as contrasted with the strictly formal, procedural rules of stage 5, and they respect human rights endangered by less mature forms of moral judgment.

A crucial consequence of this position for our purposes is what it says about justice among men, including just relationships between researchers and subjects. With respect to distributive justice, the principle of reversibility requires that the rules governing a situation be acceptable to all parties considered as free and equal, a requirement which Rawls argues can be met by the assumption that we do not know which role we will occupy in a social situation (Rawls, 1971). Applied to psychological research, this requires, among other things, that all risks that might influence participation as a subject would have to be completely acceptable to subjects as well as to investigators if both were fully informed. This requirement also indicates that deprived groups have a special claim not to have additional burdens in the form of research studies placed upon them. With respect to the human rights aspects of justice, the principle of reversibility indicates that a right always implies a duty to recognize that right in others. The rights of researchers are thus limited by the rights of subjects; and those who transgress the rights of others may make no claims to similar rights. In cases involving conflicting claims, that is, virtually all research with human subjects, the only valid solution is one consistent with recognition of the claims of all parties, subjects as well as researchers.

On the basis of this universalizable ethical theory, I would now like to comment upon specific aspects of the new APA standards for research involving human subjects.

First, cost-benefit analysis is an unsatisfactory decision-making processs, primarily because it subordinates substantive rights to benefits. By weighing benefits before risks in such a way as to frequently justify risks in terms of the social value of research, cost-benefit analysis counters the mainstream of sophisticated contemporary ethical thought, as reflected in the development of both philosophical ethics and legal opinion during the decades following the Nuremberg trials. This mainstream is perhaps best represented by the trend of federal court decisions which have increasingly stressed substantive rights, while relegating utilitarian calculations to a secondary status. The rights of citizens in cases like Miranda have increasingly been protected even where the larger society suffers, rather than benefits, from this protection. Despite recent Supreme Court appointments, this trend is continuing in the federal court system as a whole. Therefore, I would predict, on the basis of work I have been pursuing at Harvard Law School this year, that the courts will increasingly uphold the rights of subjects against investigators in suits resulting from research malpractice. And I further predict that the next revision of the APA code will place the rights of subjects above frequently vague social benefits, thereby revising the present risk-benefit recommendations.

Second, the code seriously errs in not providing a "countervailing force" against less than fully informed consent. Informed consent, other things being equal, is always desirable, because the researcher's freedom of inquiry is limited by basic liberties which require the other's consent to be abridged. This right to informed consent can *only* be violated when it is clear that everyone would agree, if they fully identified with subjects as well as researchers and citizens, that the benefits so outweigh the violation of rights as to lead everyone, if fully informed of all relevant aspects of the study, to agree to the subject's participation. This recognition of the right to fully informed consent does not rule out studies that compromise this ideal, but it requires that full weight be given to the rights and interests of the subjects at risk.

At the very least, in order to give full weight to the rights and interests of subjects, researchers should be encouraged, as part of their initial procedures, to discuss their plans with surrogate groups whenever less than fully informed consent is contemplated. By surrogate groups, I mean groups composed of representatives of the subject population. If a study of inmates in cell block A is proposed, I would require an ethical discussion with inmates in cell block B, the aim being to elicit reactions regarding potentially harmful consequences often overlooked by researchers. Surrogate groups of this sort have several advantages. They encourage the researcher to rationally justify his research before human beings with interests contrary to his own. Surrogates also often represent the interests of subjects better than the subjects themselves, because they are not overly influenced by the benefits—monetary, parole, and so on—of participation. And surrogates are less likely to uncritically assume that the researcher, as an authority figure, has their best interests in mind, especially if he presents them with his moral dilemmas. Finally, surrogates have the advantage of being able to discuss all aspects of the research without biasing the results. If every research proposal involving less than fully informed consent included a discussion of this sort, I believe researchers would spontaneously seek less objectionable ways of securing their data.

As a further means of protecting subjects from research involving less than fully informed consent, I would like to suggest that the *American Psychologist*, as the journalistic arm of the APA, adopt an editorial policy of requesting information regarding compliance with APA ethical standards in all studies submitted to it for publication. Where authors fail to satisfy this requirement, the journal would refuse to publish the unethical research findings. Presumably the importance of publishing to professional scientists would lead to a significant improvement in the ethical quality of research designs. It would also prevent the APA from implicitly sanctioning unethical projects through widespread publication of them.

Ideally, I would like to see committees established to review all research proposals involving human subjects, thereby assuring some disinterested ethical analysis not only of informed consent, but of deceit, harm, confidentiality, and so forth. Committees are also desirable, because decisions of this magnitude—involving the violation of substantive rights in favor of larger social benefits—should not be made by *any* single individual, much less an interested party. This is a societal decision of considerable importance for the moral quality of communal life which should be made by a group representative of the diverse interests involved. Neither the ethical consultations recommended by the APA nor the committees of peers required by the National Institutes of Mental Health can be expected to sufficiently represent the interests of the general public. However, representative committees must also include a high proportion of professional researchers with the appropriate expertise in order to assure scientifically informed decisions. Therefore, I recommend a committee of professionals composed in part of psychologists (some with extrainstitutional affiliations) supplemented by other behavioral scientists, a statistician to evaluate the validity of proposals, and advocates of the general public, especially lawyers and, where available, professional ethicists. Unfortunately, I am afraid this proposal is not apt to receive official APA sanction at this point in time. Nevertheless, the establishment of committees within hospital and university settings is an extremely hopeful trend.

The foregoing procedures are especially needed for research proposals involving forms of deception entailing noxious, as contrasted with trivial, behavior. Because deceptive practices not only fail to fully inform but actively manipulate and coerce behavior with lies, tricks, and other normally unacceptable devices, they are particularly troublesome. In the first place, behavior coerced by deception violates the liberty of the individual by undermining its basis in self-determination. By manipulating self-determination, deception treats other men as means, not as ends. Even when subjects eventually benefit from the study, deception, by manipulating presumably self-chosen acts to conform with the researcher's ends, denigrates their humanity. The only justification for deception is some goal—like social well-being—which everyone would agree, if they reversed roles with subjects, researchers, and citizens, warrants violation of the right not to be deceived. But this justification is especially difficult precisely because deceptive "means" necessarily result in some undesirable "ends." Among these undesirable ends, Margaret Mead rightly points not only to what deception does to subjects in terms of breaking their trust, and so on, but to what deceptive practices do to the personality of the scientist who becomes accustomed to lying, tricking, and manipulating other human beings. Dr. Mead also questions the social value of encouraging deceptive styles of research which tend to establish "a corps of progressively calloused individuals, insulated from self-criticism and increasingly . . . cynical in their manipulating of other human beings, individually and in the mass" (Mead, 1969, p. 376). Because researchers tend to assume that their knowledge of what is good for society justifies deceptive practices, it is especially necessary for codes and institutions to "lean against" violations of substantive rights involved in deceptive procedures (Ramsey, 1970, p. 79). Unfortunately, the new APA code does not sufficiently "lean against" current practices. The reason for the failure of the Ad Hoc Committee to lean against current practices is rooted in its insufficient appreciation of the priority of substantive rights. An example is the following committee comment about using deception in obtaining agreement to participate: "the ethical burden on the investigator to go ahead with (deceptive) research . . . is . . . no different in kind or mode of reasoning from other dilemmas where important scientific values are in conflict with important human values. As in other such conflicts, the situation puts the investigator in the position of weighing the pros and cons of doing the study, securing ethical guidance, and arriving at a personal decision" (Draft, May 1972, p. vii). Against this advice, universalizable principles require heavier weighting of the right not to be deceived as a constitutive aspect of the right to self-determination. Universalizable principles also indicate that deception in the initial process of gaining participation is worse than deception within an experiment to which subjects have consented knowing that they might be deceived about details. Deception about the initial contract encompasses the entire definition of the relationship, thereby inevitably undermining the moral quality of the entire interaction.

Deceptive practices involving genuine risks to physical and psychic well-being are even more disturbing. They violate not only the right to self-determination, but the right of every individual to control over, including risk-taking with, his own physical and psychic integrity as a person. Since the subject is the only person who is fully informed about his life situation and fully concerned about his personal interests, he alone should decide about the assumption of risks. Therefore, it is an extremely serious matter to subject him to risks which he may not fully understand and even worse to fail to fully persuade him of the seriousness of risks involving severe pain, anxiety, and possible long-term aftereffects in stress experiments and the like. The Ad Hoc Committee is quite correct to reserve its strongest ethical language for issues of this sort. Yet, I do not believe it has sufficiently stressed the substantive rights of subjects which, in these cases, are protected not only by ethical theory, but by law. And I certainly do not believe the committee has provided sufficient institutional safeguards. These safeguards should clearly include the employment of persons unconnected with the study to inform subjects of the risks involved. Certainly, safeguards should also include representative committees here if anywhere, for these are issues of profound ethical importance. I would not want to limit committees solely to cases involving serious risk, however, because experience has shown that it is difficult and generally unsatisfactory to require committee approval of some studies and not others.

In conclusion, I not only join Dr. Baumrind and other critics in feeling that the present code contains weaknesses and inadequacies, I also believe serious ethical reflection on the mode of reasoning employed by the Ad Hoc Committee *rationally compels* one to recognize universalizable substantive rights. These rights are compelling ethical claims in themselves, and, as such, cannot be disregarded in the name of alleged social benefits. They should be fully recognized in every decision-making procedure. Recognition of these rights calls not only for stronger principles on informed consent, deception, harm, and the like, it also necessitates institutional procedures along some of the lines briefly sketched in this paper.

BIBLIOGRAPHY

Ad Hoc Committee on Ethcal Standards in Psychological Research. *Draft of proposed principles.* Washington, D.C.: APA Monitor, 1972.

Baumrind, D. "Some thoughts on ethics of research: After reading Milgram's 'Behavioral study of obedience.'" *American Psychologist,* 1964, **19,** 421–423.

Baumrind, D. "Principles of Ethical Conduct in the Treatment of Subjects: Reaction to the Draft Report of the Committee on Ethical Standards in Psychological Research." *American Psychologist,* 1971, **26,** 887–896.

Brandt, R. B. *Ethical theory.* Englewood Cliffs, N.J.: Prentice-Hall, 1959.

Cook, S. W., Hicks, L. H., Kimble, G. A., McGuire, W. J., Schoggen, P. H., & Smith M. B. Ethical standards for research with human subjects. *APA Monitor,* May 1972, 1–29.

Dunker, Ethical relativity. *Mind,* 1939, **48,** 39–57.

Firth R. Ethical absolutism and the ideal observer. *Philosophy and phenomenological research,* 1952, **12,** 317–345.

Frankena, W. K. *Ethics.* Englewood Cliffs, N.J.: Prentice-Hall, 1963.

Freund, P. Legal framework for human experimentation. *Daedalus,* Spring 1959, 314–324.

Katz, J. *Experimentation with human beings,* New York: Russell Sage Foundation, 1972.

Jones, H. Philosophical reflections on experimenting with human subjects. *Daedalus,* Spring 1969, 219–247.

Kohlberg, L. Moral development and identification. In H. Stevenson (Ed.) Child psychology. *62nd Yearbook of the National Society for the Study of Education.* Chicago: University of Chicago Press, 1963.

Kohlberg, L. The Development of children's orientations toward a moral order: 1. Sequence in the development of moral thought. *Vita Humana,* 1963, 11–33.

Kohlberg, L. Development of moral character and ideology. In M. L. Hoffman (Ed.) *Review of Child Development Research.* Vol. 1. New York: Russell Sage Foundation, 1964.

Kohlberg, L. Cognitive stages and preschool education. *Human Development,* 1966, 5–17.

Kohlberg, L. A Cognitive developmental analysis of children's sex-role concepts and attitudes." In E. Maccoby (Ed.) *The Development of Sex Differences.* Stanford, Calif.: Stanford University Press, 1966.

Kohlberg, L. Moral and religious education and the public schools: A developmental view. In T. Sizer (Ed.) *Religion and Public Education.* Boston: Houghton-Mifflin, 1967.

Kohlberg, L. From is to ought: How to commit the naturalistic fallacy and get away with it in the study of moral development. In T. Mischel (Ed.) *Cognitive development and epistemology.* New York: Academic, 1971.

Mead, M. Research with human beings: A model derived from anthropological field practice. *Daedalus,* Spring 1969, 361–386.

Ramsey, P. *The patient as person—explorations in medical ethics.* New Haven and London: Yale University Press, 1970.

Rawls, J. "Justice as Fairness." *Philosophical Review,* 1958, **67,** 164–194.

Rawls, J. *A theory of justice.* Cambridge, Mass.: Harvard University Press, 1971.

Wallwork, E. *Durkheim: Morality and milieu.* Cambridge, Mass.: Harvard University Press, 1972.

CHAPTER 5

It neither Is nor Ought To Be: A Reply to Wallwork[*]

Diana Baumrind
University of California
Berkeley

Wallwork raises issues in his critique which are of general philosophical interest although they were introduced in the context of ethical standards for research with human subjects. I will take the opportunity to address these four issues:

1. The persuasiveness on rational grounds of deontological systems of justification
2. The role of tautology in rhetoric, and of formal logic in moral discourse
3. The factual basis for Wallwork's claim that basic disagreements concerning ethical standards are resolvable at stage 6 of moral reasoning
4. Personal versus public justification of moral values

[*] The author while preparing this paper was supported in part by the National Institute of Child Health and Human Development under Research Grant HD 02228.

THE PERSUASIVENESS ON RATIONAL GROUNDS OF DEONTOLOGICAL SYSTEMS OF JUSTIFICATION

The deontological system of justification as presented by Wallwork is intrinsically nonempirical and therefore nonpersuasive. Neither does it facilitate the formulation of sound arguments more than would a teleological system.

Wallwork defends his position on the basis that it is more objective and consistent than the teleological position I defend. I will show that it is not. Moreover his arguments tend to be circular and equivocal. Frequently Wallwork presents his arguments in the conditional tense and then draws his conclusion as though he had been referring to the truth of fact in (1) a real world or (2) in all possible worlds. For example, in justifying his two substantive rules Wallwork says, "These substantive rules are universalizable because every rational moral agent, as a matter of reflective policy, could agree...." Is Wallwork's proposition intended as a tautologous statement or as a testable hypothesis? We would have to agree that the proposition Wallwork proposes *could* be true. But then almost any proposition "could" be true, or for that matter "could not" be true. For reasoning to be persuasive it must be testable, not merely tautologous. To be testable, Wallwork would have to substitute "would" or "would probably" where he says "could." If "would" is substituted for "could," Wallwork's argument can be rebutted by any single negative case since it pertains to *every* rational moral agent. I am an example of a negative case in that I cannot agree with his first substantive principle, namely that "persons are of unconditional value." As a first principle, I find as persuasive the contrary proposition that "The Tao is of universal value while the person is of value to the degree that his way conforms with the Tao" or the alternative proposition: "All life forms are of unconditional value." But in fact all such statements concerning the value of persons sound rather fatuous. Faced by the empirical reality of my disagreement with one of his fundamental substantive moral principles, Wallwork could argue, I suppose, that I am incapable of stage 6 reasoning, and therefore am not sufficiently rational, moral, or reflective for him to take my case seriously. He could even prove logically such an assertion by the construction of an appropriate tautology such as:

Only persons who accept the two substantive moral principles—(1) persons are of unconditional value, and (2) persons have the right to equal justice in all situations—are capable of stage 6 reasoning and qualify as rational, moral, reflective beings.

Baumrind rejects principle (1).

Therefore, Baumrind is not capable of stage 6 reasoning and does not qualify as a rational, moral, and reflective being.

But then I would refuse to grant the truth of his major premise. By what principle then would Wallwork justify substantive principle (1) which I reject?

I have attended carefully to Wallwork's arguments. Yet I have not been convinced. R. S. Peters (1971) and W. P. Alston (1971) paid careful attention to Kohlberg's (1971) arguments and they were not convinced. The deontological contention that all rational, moral men upon reflection "would" agree, is disproven by these facts. If the contention is that they "could" agree, there can be no argument since that empty statement can neither be confirmed nor rejected.

Wallwork accuses me of subjectivity. He appears to believe that rhetoric concerning moral issues should be limited to establishing logical connections between beliefs solely on the basis of reason. If indeed Wallwork thinks that "crucial statements throughout her [Baumrind's] paper beg the real issues in favor of what I call 'justification by personal reference'—as exemplified by sentences beginning with 'I believe'" then Wallwork must think that crucial statements of his own "beg the real issues," e.g., his statement "I *feel* it is incumbent upon me to do this, as I *believe* psychologists are rationally compelled to formulate stronger ethical standards for research involving human subjects and to monitor these principles more rigorously" (italics mine). What can be more subjective than intuitionism? Yet that is how Wallwork and Kohlberg justify the superiority of stage 6 reasoning. Exactly two susbtantive principles are formulated by Kohlberg and presented here by Wallwork as the basis on which stage 6 reasoning is superior to stage 5 reasoning. From where do these particular two principles arise? Wallwork states that these two principles could be universalized and are explicitly demonstrable at stage 6 reasoning. Yet there is empirical evidence that not all highly sophisticated thinkers do in fact agree; i.e., the intuitionist statement that "all rational moral agents upon reflection would agree" with these two principles is false. Nietzsche is a case in point. Does Wallwork really think that Nietzsche's argument (or Ayn Rand's) on behalf of ethical egoism reflects inability to understand the principle of reversibility? Or that Marx's justification of the rights of the exploited class above those of the exploiter class reflects an inability to put himself in the place of the class enemy? Would Wallwork contend that Zen masters, who reject on principle substantive moral principles (and instead require of the disciple zazen, i.e., *practice*) are incapable of understanding the formal operational logic they reject? Are we to believe that all theologians who defend submission to God as an act of faith are incapable of postconventional reasoning?

The ultimate justification of rule-utilitarianism (or ethical universalism as it is sometimes called) is in theory empirical rather than intuitional. Rule-utilitarians take the position that the ultimate end is the greatest general good and claim that by following certain rules under appropriate and specified circumstances that end can be achieved. The ultimate justification of deontological systems is, by contrast, nonempirical and therefore not testable. Wallwork equivocates on the relevance of empirical proof. He argues both for the logical superiority and the empirical validity of the Kohlberg system. When for rhetorical purposes the nonempirical "could" is changed to "would" and empirical claims are made for the universality of the system Wallwork supports, the evidence presented is not persuasive (see the Section, "The Factual Basis of Wallwork's Claim . . ."). Wallwork's arguments for the rational superiority of the system are not valid either.

Wallwork's logical arguments on behalf of the universalist ethic are circular. That is, he assumes the truth of what he sets out to prove. According to Wallwork, the validity of his position "depends not upon the empirical validity of his developmental theory, but upon the logical superiority of stage 6 moral reasoning to stage 5." Wallwork states that "One basic problem with stage 5 moral reasoning which relates to the new code is its failure to justify an independent ethical stance against group rules that sanction or permit the violation of fundamental human rights. . . . When conflicts between group rules and fundamental rights as well as among diverse group rules arise, morally sensitive men feel compelled to move beyond the confines of the formal contractual and rule-utilitarian orientations of stage 5." What is the *logic* which compels "morally sensitive" men to embrace Wallwork's substantive principles? What is there about "morally sensitive" men which compels them to be logical in the first place? Wallwork tries to prove that "morally sensitive men feel compelled to move beyond the confines of the formal contractual and rule-utilitarian orientations of stage 5," by arguing that the stage 5 subject is in a bind because he cannot justify "an independent ethical stance against group rules that sanction or permit the violation of fundamental human rights." But is that not the conclusion he is trying to prove, namely that the stage 5 person will feel required by the logic of his position to justify an *independent* ethical stance against group rules? Similarly, Kohlberg (1971) assumes that the stage 5 person will feel required to arrive at a "stable state of equilibrium" and is in a bind because he cannot do so with stage 5 reasoning (p. 205). But I contend that stage 5 reasoning is as stable as stage 6 reasoning; the person who has achieved stage 5 reasoning should feel no need to resort to stage 6 reasoning in order to reject group consensus. He need merely claim that the rule he follows which happens to differ from group consensus enhances the common good despite the group consensus that it does not. He is not required by stage 5 logic to justify his independent stand just because not all other rational beings could or do agree.

There are inconsistencies in Wallwork's position in addition to those already mentioned:

1. Wallwork's claim that stage 5 reasoning is limited to a consideration of procedural rules would appear to contradict Kohlberg's (1971) claim that constitutional democracy, a stage 5 invention, includes a specific list of substantive rights, i.e., the Bill of Rights. It is true that the two substantive rights which Wallwork proposes are more abstract, but it is not true that they are somehow more substantive, more intuitively given, more logical or more factually solid, than rights derivable from a rule-utilitarian rationale such as are contained in the Bill of Rights.

2. Wallwork's use of the term "universal" is equivocal. If by universal is meant "found in every culture," then stages 1–4 are universal and stages 5 and 6 are not. Certainly self-interest is a more universally found value than the two principles Wallwork and Kohlberg

propose. If by universal is meant "universalizable" (i.e., could be universalized), then we are dealing only in conjecture. Every proposition for which universalizability is claimed either "could"' or "could not" be true, a very empty claim indeed.

3. Within the logic of the system Wallwork espouses, one stage is defined as higher than another on the basis of formal criteria of structural adequacy with the exception of the transition from stage 5 to stage 6. Using the same logic, there appears to be no way to justify the sudden switch from formal to substantive criteria. Stage 6 reasoning is not more differentiated or more integrated than stage 5 reasoning. It merely has appended to it two specific (and by no means universally acceptable) substantive beliefs whose function presumably is to justify the protection of fundamental human rights. It is assumed, contrary to fact, that these rights are not otherwise justifiable. But fundamental human rights could just as well be justified by appeal to the common good. Why the protection of fundamental human rights *ought* to take precedence if their protection could not be justified by appeal to the long-range common good is also unexplained.

4. Prior to the "final" stage, transition from one stage to another is said by Piaget and Kohlberg to take place by dialectical transformation brought about by disequilibrium and the individual's attempt to reach a stable state of equilibrium. Suddenly when the individual reaches stage 6 he has "arrived" and from now on he can live comfortably ever after in a state of stable equilibrium. Why should movement and progression characterize human thought up to a point but no further? Until stage 6 we see the old replaced by the new (negation) and the new replaced by the synthesis which reinstates aspects of both the thesis and the antithesis (negation of the negation). Suddenly this dialectical progression is halted. Why the "final stage" should be reached before the "final solution" is inexplicable within the Kohlberg system, and to my way of thinking would be wholly undesirable if it were possible.

Since Wallwork views stage 6 as final and his presumed attainment of stage 6 reasoning as desirable, it is unlikely that he would be motivated to recognize a "higher" stage of reasoning than his own. Wallwork may be willing to concede, however, that others have believed that they perceived a stage of existence which was higher than that defined by stage 6 reasoning—i.e., a postmoral and postrational stage of existence. Kierkegaard, for example, regards the highest form of existence to be antirational and antimoral. He classifies intellectuals as adhering to the first developed form, namely the esthetic, in which the good is defined as "the desired." He regards the next highest form of existence as that in which man lives according to universal moral norms, or what Wallwork and Kohlberg might regard as stage 6 obligations. The third or highest form of existence according to Kierkegaard is where man commits himself by a leap of faith to act against his rational understanding or personal desires. Consider also the famous *gatha* of Jenye, a Zen master living in the fifth century A.D.:

> Empty-handed I go, and behold the spade is in my hands;
> I walk on foot, and yet on the back of an ox I am riding;
> When I pass over the bridge,
> Lo, the water floweth not, but the bridge doth flow.

This statement so often quoted by Zen Masters such as Suzuki (1964, p. 58) exemplifies rejection of logic as a way of gaining knowledge. Jung is in accord with the Zen masters when he says that in the highest state of consciousness, differentiation yields to merging; the well-differentiated ego merges with nature in old age.

As these examples illustrate, there is a way of viewing value judgments which may transcend the particular negation of the negation contained within the Kohlberg system. In order to move beyond stage reasoning it may be necessary to reject noncontradictory logic and the particular stages which Kohlberg sees as invariant and sufficient.

5. Wallwork argues that only stage 6 universalist reasoning can be used to justify the protection of human rights. But the arguments he resorts to in order to justify the protection of fundamental human rights seldom contain stage 6 reasoning. For example, he argues that the cost-benefit analysis "counters the mainstream of sophisticated contemporary ethical thought . . . best represented by the trend of federal court decisions." This is either stage 3 or stage 4 reasoning depending upon whether he wishes us to affiliate with the good guys, i.e., the "sophisticates," or wishes us to conform with the current definition of law. (If his argument were based on due process he would not refer us to a "trend.") I disagree with his factual statement that the rights of citizens have increasingly been protected even where the larger society suffers, and I also disagree about whether

they should be so protected if indeed the larger society would suffer as a consequence. In any event my judgment, and Wallwork's, will have to made independent from the judgment of even the highest court if we are to view ourselves as resorting to postconventional reasoning. For another example, Wallwork states that the "only justification for deception is some goal—like social well-being." He further emphasizes that the effects of deceptive practices have harmful *consequences* on the personalities of subjects and researchers alike, which is the same rule-utilitarian justification which he purports to reject as insufficient. Instead if he were to adhere to his deontological stance, Wallwork would argue that deceptive practices are harmful because they violate the unconditional value of each human being. A third example is that Wallwork resorts to the use of consensus, due process, and the committee system to determine whether in a given instance "the benefits so outweight the violation of rights as to lead everyone, if fully informed of all relevant aspects of the study, to agree to the subject's participation." But what attribute could the "benefits" possess from the viewpoint of a deontologist which could outweigh violation of the fundamental human rights of subjects? Also, if the committee is composed of the subject's peers and these peers have not yet reached the postconventional level, how can their decision based upon a cost-benefit analysis be moral from the viewpoint of a stage 6 thinker? Does the fact that a committee decides "in favor of larger social benefits" over "the violation of substantive rights" justify that decision to a stage 6 thinker? Additionally, Wallwork proposes various forms of coercion which authorities in the American Psychological Association could use to "persuade" recalcitrant professional scientists to raise their stage of moral reasoning. thus appealing to stage 2 motives to move his colleagues.

While I am not persuaded by deontological universalist thinking and continue to assert that "Differences based upon genuinely contradictory world-views are not resolvable," I also hold that most actual disagreements concerning moral conduct do not involve fundamental metaethical issues, and are resolvable. Even persons who disagree on world-views can frequently agree upon a common action, i.e., they consider the relevant facts, examine carefully the prudential bases of their disagreement, and search for a compromised position based upon common interest. In my original paper I stated that disagreements concerning practical ethical judgments may arise from a number of sources which I listed in order of their susceptibility to resolution. It appears to me that most of my disagreements with the committee concern more easily resolved issues such as (1) factual disagreements concerning the probable effects of a given action, (2) differences as to how a rule in a given instance should be applied, and (3) differences in the relative weights assigned to rules on which we both place a positive value, *rather than* less resolvable issues such as (4) disagreements as to the direction assigned a given rule, (5) differing views concerning the nature of good and evil, (6) incompatible theories of justification, or (7) fundamental differences in worldview. Our differences therefore should be resolvable in practice as well as in principle unless their bases are predominantly emotional or prudential. It is reasonable to point out (and may be persuasive) that the qualifications to the principles enunciated in the APA Code of Ethics destroy the credibility of the principles themselves. In order to justify the inclusion of these principles, it is necessary to subvert the reasoning used to defend the principles. Recourse to deontological reasoning, however, is neither required to produce a sound argument against the cost-benefit analysis nor persuasive on rational or affective grounds. On the contrary, the either/or form of argument to which deontologists resort, and their intolerant and parochial denigration of so-called lower-level thinking motivates adversaries to strenghten their own arguments and impedes honest dialogue.

THE ROLE OF TAUTOLOGY IN RHETORIC, AND OF FORMAL LOGIC IN MORAL DISCOURSE

A valid argument is not necessarily a sound argument. Arguments which are true only by virtue of their logical form are not persuasive.

Wallwork, like Piaget, relies heavily on noncontradictory logical criteria to substantiate his system of justification. Wallwork does not seem conversant with reasoning which relies on dialectical rather than formal logic. Wozniak (1973), among other philosopher-psychologists, regards formal Aristotelian logic as insufficient to cope with the complexities of psychological or historical relationships. Hegelian logic explicitly rejects the *law of the excluded middle* on which Aristotelian logic is based, affirming instead that A is always *becoming* non-*A*. The noncontradictory thinking which Wallwork and Kohlberg regard as superior and characteristic of stage 6 thinkers is by no means universally accepted. Rather, it is viewed as misleading and insufficient by quite "sophisticated" dialectical philosophers.

A logically sound argument cannot be constructed using ambiguous terms. All terms are to some extent ambiguous in the sense that they shift their meaning with the circumstances. A term as used in the premise may not be identical with that term as used in the conclusion or with itself in another time or place. The truth of a proposition affirmed under one set of circumstances may have to be rejected when the circumstances change. Even such a "clear" premise as "I am hot" is both true and not true. Am I always hot? By comparison with what or whom am I hot? Am I identical with myself? And so on. Value judgments consist of claims about what is of worth—what is good, what is just, what is beautiful. A statement of fact (such as "I am hot") is an empirical statement about which universal agreement is possible in principle (although not in reality), by contrast with a statement of values which is not. Value terms such as beauty, truth, or justice cannot be defined univocally. Their meaning varies with the individual's preferences, bound within the matrix of cultural and historical context. If a simple statement of fact such as "I am hot" shifts in meaning, how is it conceivable that a moral statement such as "Each life is of unconditional value" could be designated as either true or false for all time, in all places, and under all circumstances. The place of formal logic in inference is limited by the fact that *A* is always *becoming* non-*A*. It has little or no place in inferences involving terms where *A is* also non-*A*.

When Wallwork says "Dr. Baumrind seems driven by the logic of her second line of reasoning to the unsatisfactory emotivist position that ethical claims are merely reflections of subjective desires . . . ," he is committing the all or nothing fallacy; i.e., he is making the mistake of denying the truth inherent both in a position *and* in its contradiction. I would no more contend that "ethical claims are *merely* reflections of subjective desires" than I would contend that ethical claims are *merely* reflections of rational cognitions. The strongest *rational* appeal in an argument with an advocate who disagrees fundamentally with your ethical judgments is to show him that the logical or factual consequences of his position are self-defeating *within his own system of values*. But nonrational appeals are also entirely appropriate in disputes concerning ethical conduct. Nonrational appeals are not *merely* "ethical ejaculations." In order to convince an adversary, appeals to extralogical connections urged by emotion, self-interest, religious experience, historical necessity, and aesthetics are all appropriate. There is nothing disreputable, deceptive, or immature about such appeals. It is true, as Wallwork suggests, that my arguments arise from my personal system of justification, as well as from my public system of justification, and that arguments derived from a personal need not be logically compelling. They may however be persuasive on other grounds (see the section, "Personal versus Public Justification of Moral Values"). When Wallwork states that I appeal in my rhetoric to extralogical connections he is correct. Certainly he would not claim that he does otherwise.

By logical deduction or inference we refer to an intellectual process in which some things are judged to be true by virtue of their relations to other items of belief. In logical discourse a sound argument is one with *true* premises which constitute sufficient grounds for asserting the conclusion. A valid argument is one in which the conclusion must be true *if* the premises are true. A valid argument is not necessarily a sound argument. It is always possible to escape the conclusion of any argument, i.e., to deny its soundness by refusing to assent to the material truth of the premises. Following are four valid arguments whose conclusions I reject by denying the material truth of the first premise:

1. All democrats are subversive.
   McGovern is a democrat.
   Therefore, McGovern is subversive.

2. All rational, moral agents agree that persons are of unconditional value.
   Baumrind does not agree that persons are of unconditional value.
   Therefore, Baumrind is not a rational, moral agent.

3. If a universal morality cannot be found on which all men in principle agree, men are free to violate the fundamental human rights of others.
   No such universal morality can be found.

Therefore, men are free to violate the fundamental human rights of others.

4. Either each man's life is judged as of equal value to every other man's life or murder will occur.
Murder is to be prevented.
Therefore, each man's life must be judged to be of equal value to every other man's life.

It is my observation that where the material truth of the concluding proposition is not granted, the material truth of at least one premise will also be rejected. That is, unless the conclusion "proven" by the relation between the premises is acknowledged as true even without justification, the justification offered will not prove persuasive. But, if the conclusion is so acknowledged, then no disagreement exists to be resolved.

It is not possible to justify moral principles on logical grounds alone. Yet this is exactly what Wallwork attempts to do by claiming that the two substantive principles he proposes "derive from this search for universalizability." But suppose:

1. I reject the search for universalizability as a desideratum

or

2. I accept the search for universalizability as a desideratum but reject the specific two principles which Wallwork and Kohlberg propose in favor of others (such as those proposed earlier in this paper)

By what chain of reasoning am I then to be persuaded to share Wallwork's fondness for "universalizability" as a criterion, or his two principles as ultimate values? Wallwork's theory here is really circular and explains nothing. It is in the form of "Since p then p." I simply reject p. His argument for the superiority of stage 6 reasoning is tautological; i.e., his fundamental statements in support of the logical superiority of stage 6 are definitional and devoid of empirical content. A tautologous statement is one which is necessarily true by virtue either of its meaning, e.g., "All virgins are celibate," or its form, e.g., "It rained yesterday or it did not rain yesterday." While any chain of reasoning that is an instance of tautology is correct by virtue of its form, that chain of reasoning is not necessarily sound. Thus a tautologous statement is not sound and cannot enter into theory building if empirical data offered in opposition to it must support it. The contention that only individuals capable of stage 6 reasoning will intuitively perceive its superiority is an example of a tautologous statement which should not be used in theory building.

As I have tried to show in this section, neither appeal to logic nor universalist ethics can banish indeterminancy in moral discourse. A formal science such as pure mathematics is concerned only with whether in an argument the conclusion is entailed by the premises. An empirical science is also concerned with the truth of the premises. To paraphrase Albert Einstein's comment on mathematics, "As far as the laws of morality refer to reality, they are not universalizable; and as far as they are universalizable, they do not refer to reality." (Einstein said "mathematics" where we say "morality" and "certain" where we say "universalizable.") This does not mean that rational criteria cannot be applied to value judgments, even to judgments involving fundamental differences. Most value judgments rest not merely on subjective attitudes but also on factual presuppositions. Empirical evidence can be brought to bear which will confirm or reject factual presuppositions, and in that way alter value judgments.

THE FACTUAL BASIS FOR WALLWORK'S CLAIM THAT BASIC DISAGREEMENTS CONCERNING ETHICAL STANDARDS ARE RESOLVABLE AT STAGE 6 OF MORAL REASONING

Kohlberg's research does not demonstrate that disagreements among philosophers are resolvable.

I would like now to discuss Wallwork's claim that "Kohlberg's research explicitly demonstrates that the disagreements she [Baumrind] cites between philosophers, like Kant and Mill, . . . are theoretically resolvable at the highest stage of moral reasoning, stage 6 (Kohlberg, 1971, pp. 163–180)." The *data* referred to in those pages explicitly demonstrate no such thing. For a summary of the cross-cultural data to which Wallwork alludes, I refer the reader to figure 1 on page 172 and to figure 2 on page 173 of the Kohlberg (1971) article Wallwork cites. These data demonstrate that among middle-class urban boys in Taiwan and Mexico, stage 3 reasoning predominates by age 16, and that it is only among middle-class urban *boys* in the United States that stage 5 reasoning predominates. In two other villages, stage 1 remains the modal stage of moral reasoning by the same age, and postconventional thinking is entirely absent. By what logic do these cross-cultural data support Wallwork's claim that cultural differences are resolvable at the highest stage of moral reasoning? None of the subjects cited even reached that stage. It should also be noted that Kohlberg's new scoring manual supercedes the manual used to score the cross-cultural data. When data are presented by critics based upon the old manual, Kohlberg frequently objects on the basis that there are discrepancies between the new and the old scoring. Data based on the "old" system of scoring presumably should not be cited as conclusive by any investigator, including Wallwork, even if (contrary to fact) these data were to support Wallwork's assertions of universality and universability. There are at present in press or preparation a number of papers challenging Kohlberg's assumptions of stage invariance, irreversability, and universality on empirical grounds (e.g., Holstein, 1973; Kurtines & Greif, 1974). We may expect others. There is then substantial reason to question Wallwork's claims that Kohlberg's factual data explicitly demonstrate the validity of his universalist claims.

I believe that were a debate to be staged among sophisticated members representing such divergent viewpoints as Zen Buddhism, secular existentialism, Christianity, Kantian ethics, Marxism, and rule-utiltarianism, it would quickly become apparent that there were in fact irreconcilable differences concerning criteria for defining, and justifying the definition of the "good life." That is because what constitutes a good life is in fact historically conditioned and, to some extent, subjective.

An additional problem with using Kohlberg's research to buttress arguments concerned with ethical *conduct* is that it deals with reasoning about interpersonal issues, and not with moral conduct. What is prescriptive in action for an individual is of course affected by his level of moral judgment—but how much so is another question. What a person thinks ought to be done and what he thinks *he* ought to do are not identical. What he thinks he ought to do may not determine either what he *would* do or how he would *judge himself* if he did otherwise. The resolution of moral conflict in real life is a profoundly emotional experience, as well as a cognitively demanding one. Yet the moral dilemma situations which comprise the Kohlberg interview are constructed in such a way as to minimize the respondent's identification with the plight of the participants and thus his emotional involvement. The locus is intentionally foreign, and the characters are quaint and old-fashioned. The subject is encouraged to talk about what the story characters should do, and not what he—the subject—would or should do. The situations themselves are unreal exactly because they are structured as dilemmas. In real life a person conducts himself morally by preventing the occurrence of dilemmas or situations in which an *important* moral principle must be violated to bring about a higher good. The either/or options which such Kohlberg characters as Heinz and Joe face are unreal since most actual situations of ethical conflict can be resolved without choosing this *or* that option. It is not likely therefore that subjects' responses to the Kohlberg moral dilemma stories predict their responses in actual situations requiring moral choices any better than a nonmoral test of developmental maturity. The fact that the story line in the moral dilemmas requires the subjects to deal with such issues as prescriptivity and possibly universality does not mean that these judgments *about* morality engage the moral faculties. To my knowledge there has been no test of the hypothesis that respondents' scores on any established test of *nonmoral* maturity measuring cognitive, emotional, or esthetic maturity (e.g., Loevinger's test of ego development, Stanford-Binet MA, or Piaget's logico-mathematical tests) would predict moral conduct as well or better than scores on Kohlberg's test of moral maturity. By excluding other dimensions of moral character such as compassion, altruism, autonomy and moral knowledge, Kohlberg may merely be assessing cognitive maturity, using items whose content is limited to moral issues.

Despite these important qualifications, significant relationships can be shown to exist between level of moral judgment—as measured by the Kohlberg scores—and level of moral conduct. These significant correlations between judgment and action are to be expected since both judgment and action are part of a causal chain which includes the effects of factors such as intelligence, social class, early childhood experiences, affective state, and group values. The relationship between judgment and action should be higher at lower levels of reasoning since if a person judges that he is obliged to act as his desires at the moment dictate, his judgment as to how he should act and his action should coincide.

At higher levels, larger discrepancies are to be expected. There are several factors which could account for these discrepancies when they occur. First, conventional or postconventional reasoning urges discretion, distancing, and concern for others—all of which require self-control and invite frustration. Second, a person capable of sophisticated formal reasoning is also capable of formulating valid arguments to rationalize such discrepancies. Third, a person capable of sophisticated formal reasoning may be motivated to exercise his ability to deceive and manipulate others—it is a pity to let such an amusing and useful ability atrophy through disuse. Therefore, raising a person's level of moral judgment by enabling him to rationalize his behavior using postconventional reasoning may actually facilitate the enactment on his part of preconventional conduct, provided that he is motivated to act immorally and "get away with it." It is this very phenomenon which argues against raising the general level of moral reasoning without at the same time providing a strong rationale for bringing moral conduct into conformity with moral reasoning. The possible negative consequences of establishing a code of ethics in which ethical principles are clearly formulated but a parallel system of rationalizations established which condones conduct in violation of these principles may well be to encourage such immoral conduct.

The idea that empirical research concerned with moral judgment could conceivably resolve basic disagreements concerning the nature of good and evil is manifestly absurd. Research experiments cannot lead to absolute truth but only to relative truth, dependent upon the conditions set up by the scientist himself. Surely Wallwork would not deny that the Heisenberg principle applies to research concerned with what *is* or *ought* to be. Even in his investigations of the objective physical world, man cannot escape the limitations imposed by the measurement process. Can he imagine that by viewing the other as object he could avoid finding himself in the way?

PERSONAL VERSUS PUBLIC JUSTIFICATION OF MORAL VALUES

There is a dialectical relationship between the existential needs of man for maximum individuation and autonomy, and the social needs of the communal living group for conformity to authority and/or peer consensus.

Man is a social animal, but he is not *merely* a social animal! The human personality must be considered in relation to the social and historical spheres which shape it and in turn are shaped by it, and also in relation to the transcendental realities which the mind constructs and in turn by which it is constructed. By "transcendent" I refer to the person's apprehension that there is a level of understanding at which elements now seen as disparate and irreconcilable belong to the same system and obey the same laws. The transcendental experience of Unity, in which the constituent elements of the universe are experienced as manifestations of a single principle, constitutes the basic mystical "insight" and may characterize all religious feeling. Man's conviction that such a synthesis exists, even if he has had no personal experience with "enlightenment," can be defended rationally (although as faith it need not be) on the ground that revolutions in thought have actually occurred that did create such a novel synthesis which prior to the qualitative leap in thought was apprehended without being comprehended. The outcome of each such revolution in thought was to give man control over what heretofore had "happened" to him as if by magic. But if man's knowledge increases arithmetically, his apprehension of what there is to know increases exponentially. Thus the vision of a superordinate synthesis beyond man's grasp abides, and most men are happy to enjoy that vision and embellish it with constructed fictions and suspended disbeliefs. Or the individual may embrace his myth as literal reality.

When metaphysical convictions take the form of *faith* in God or nature, all goes well. The generative source is seen as outside the self and equally available to all men. The believer will not presume to any special knowledge of good and evil, and therefore engage in evangelical crusades. The ecumenical movement serves a function in discouraging such crusades.

But if the individual presumes to special *knowledge* of good and evil all may not go well; more often than not the enlightened individual believes that access to this special knowledge justifies antinomian behavior. The emphasis on knowledge, rather than faith, as the means for attaining salvation, or even as the form of salvation itself, and the claim that one's own articulated doctrine expresses this knowledge is called "Gnosticism." The "Knowing One" may imagine that his special knowledge is of God, or he may imagine that it is of natural reality. What characterizes the Gnostic is not that he acts on his convictions but that he justifies the actions which they generate on the basis that these personal revelations yield *true knowledge*, and morever that *only an elect few can be initiated into that knowledge*. His claim is self-fulfilling since to deny it is to identify oneself as ignorant of true knowledge. True knowledge is perfect and immutable. Direct access through intuition to true knowledge places the Gnostic beyond the social definition of good and evil. He has been transformed by his revelations into Good itself, and thus stands above the law, a law unto himself. Nonconformism is a principle of the Gnostic mind and is a way of bearing witness to the truth. The spirit acting as a source of direct knowledge and illumination reigns sovereign. The pneumatic or free spirit is liberated from the yoke of moral law; to him all things are permitted. Hail the antinomian: he has attained stage 6!

I object to certain provisions of the APA Code of Ethics and to Wallwork's stage theory claims to higher gnosis because in both instances the other is asked to accept the advocate's values as his own, not on faith or contingent upon the presentation of evidence, but because the advocate claims special insight as a result of his privileged position as a scientist, or alternatively his presumed ascent to stage 6 morality. The Gnostic heresy revisited is called in current vernacular, "Laying Your Trip on Others."

The demands of the Inward and the Outward are different, and sometimes contradictory. The common good may require of most men, that where there is a conflict that they abide by their public rather than their personal values, *and* of a few men that they do not. Even if that is true, there can be no justification for elevating the value hierarchy of the few over the value hierarchy of the many.

There is a way of reconciling the demands of conscience and the common good where these seem to conflict. It is to contend that the worth of the individual's work is greater than the harm he does and that a condition of his productivity is that he act in accord with his conscience. However no individual is sufficiently objective to contend that about himself. Even if the common good were to be abetted by some persons placing their duty to themselevs above the common good it is better for the common good that the individual simply act in accord with his personal conscience or duty to himself and not try to justify his choice.

The conflict between the claims of conscience and the communal good is perennial. I regard such conflicts as dilemmas and myself as culpable whichever choice I make since dilemmas are at all times to be avoided. The choice in favor of conscience is a choice in favor of ego. That choice in favor of ego cannot be justified by a teleological system of ethics such as rule-utilitarianism but could be by a deontological system such as Kant's. But for rule-utilitarian reasons I refuse to justify ethical egoism by deontological reasoning. As a system of moral philosophy, Ethical Egoism is self-contradictory. In order to be valid it would require a social harmony which does not exist. If all individuals defined their welfare in terms of authenticity and self-realization, ethical egoism might be a tenable system. But since most persons define their welfare in terms of primary needs, the egoistic maxim, were it to be generalized, would not be to my advantage. Therefore logically I cannot will the egoistic maxim to be a general law.

With Kant (1963) I choose to regard my duty to myself as constituting the supreme condition of my morality and to act in accord with that choice. But I will not universalize my hierarchy of values nor justify my choice when its results proved injurious to others. Kierkegaard believed that any act against reason or love committed by a Knight of Faith in service of the Absolute was by virtue of that bondage justified. Without belief in the absolute the Knight of Faith and demonic man are one. By rejecting belief in the absolute, I forego the security of public justification.

In closing, I want to comment briefly on Brewster's observation that I set myself a task different from the task which the committee set for itself in formulating the APA Code of Ethics. When Wallwork says that "Dr. Smith implicitly recognizes this failure in rational persuasion when he dismisses Dr. Baumrind's ethical philosophy as a personal statement," I think that he completely misunderstands the point of Dr. Smith's observation. Dr. Smith is pointing out that the outcome of an argument is determined by neither party but occurs as a consequence of interaction between two fully articulated but divergent positions and perspectives. Smith is saying that the outcome in terms of raising the level of ethical discourse is served best by interaction between formulator, critic, and conciliator. Smith prefers the role of conciliator and I the role of critic. He does not find it necessary to denigrate my role in the dispute, nor I his, for each of us to enact that role to the full. Since neither one of us imagines that there is a best solution, nor that the other takes one stance because he is incapable of arguing from another stance, we are both content to play out our respectives roles—I as critic and he as conciliator. With Dr. Smith I believe that truth is a product of the confrontations of divergent interests and value perspectives and not the unique creation of a few highly developed individuals. This view of truth as a human product brought into being by the interactions among individuals, each conditioned by his own experience and limited by his place in history, is antithetical to the universalists' search for a determined and eternally valid ethical imperative.

BIBLIOGRAPHY

Alston, W. P. Comments on Kohlberg's "From is to ought." In T. Mischel (Ed.), *Cognitive development and epistemology*. New York: Academic, 1971.

Holstein, C. B. Moral judgment change in early adolescence and middle age: A longitudinal study. Paper presented at the Biennial Meeting of the Society for Research in Child Development, Philadelphia, March 29–April 1, 1973.

Kant, I. *Lectures on ethics*. New York: Harper & Row, 1963.

Kohlberg, L. From is to ought: How to commit the naturalistic facllacy and get away with it in the study of moral development. In T. Mischel (Ed.), *Cognitive development and epistemology*. New York: Academic, 1971.

Kurtines, W., & Greif, E. B. The development of moral thought: A review and evaluation of Kohlberg's approach. To be published in *Psychological Bulletin*, Fall, 1974.

Peters, R. S. Moral developments. A plea for pluralism. In T. Mischel (Ed.), *Cognitive development and epistemology*. New York: Academic, 1971.

Suzuki, D. T. *An introduction to Zen Buddhism*. New York: Grove, 1964.

Wozniak, R. H. Structuralism, dialectical materialism, and cognitive developmental theory: An examination of certain basic assumptions of Piagetian theory. Paper presented at the Biennial Meeting of the Society for Research in Child Development, Philadelphia, March 1973.

CHAPTER 6

In Defense of Substantive Rights: A Reply to Baumrind

Ernest Wallwork

Yale University
New Haven

The issues involved in the debate between Baumrind and myself could scarcely be more important. Nothing less is at stake than the justification of everyday moral arguments, the meaning and claim of justice in human affairs, and the specific problem of ethically proper procedures for research involving human subjects. In view of the seriousness of these issues and the sharpness of Baumrind's critique, I propose to respond to each of her major points in the order in which they are raised in "It Neither Is Nor Ought To Be." This procedure has the advantage of clarifying the issues upon which we disagree, despite its principal disadvantage of mixing questions of fact, meta-ethics, normative theory, and casuistry, issues which I shall attempt to distinguish as they arise.

Initially, it is sufficient to note that many of the arguments in this response either repudiate or seriously modify Baumrind's reading of my first paper. I am frankly not surprised, given the 15-minute limitation on my reactions at the Loyola symposium, that Baumrind found several points where it was not precisely clear which of several possible meanings I had in mind. What is surprising is her decision to compensate for ambiguities and brevity by attributing to me ideas—like intuitionism, ethical logicalism, and monistic deontology—that I nowhere suggest. Equally surprising is the frequency with which ideas are attributed to Kohlberg and to me that we have both explicitly refuted in widely available publications.

I

Baumrind construes my statement that "every rational moral agent, as a matter of reflective policy, *could* agree that in similar situations each is to be respected and to be accorded the claims of equal justice" as a tautology which could or could not be true. In fact, I use "could" in this context, as Kohlberg uses it, in the sense of "would be possible" given the specific conditions necessary for mature moral development, conditions which, when fully realized, also assure the validity of moral judgments (see section VI of this paper). These conditions include attainment of Piaget's cognitive stage of formal operations, impartial and sympathetic role-taking capacities, and critical reflection (involving generalization, consistency, conceptual clarity, and adequate information) on the problem of adjudicating disparate claims regarding the rights and duties, burdens and benefits, powers and immunities of social existence. No tautology is entailed in claiming that men in all societies "could" logically and consistently agree, given these conditions, that each is to be respected and to be accorded the claims of equal justice. Far from being an empty claim, Kohlberg's evidence in support of this position challenges the relativist assertion that moral disagreements are irreconcilable and, thereby, lends credence to the stronger metaethical thesis that, under ideal epistemological circumstances, all men "would" agree to these principles. In retrospect, my remarks were not as clear as they should have been regarding this distinction between the factual possibility of agreement and the metaethical criteria for establishing the truth of ethical claims. But this ambiguity existed because Kohlberg's final stage incorporates ideal epistemological conditions that assure that all men

In Defense of Substantive Rights 105

"would" agree to the principles of equal respect and justice (see sections VI and VIII). With regard to the factual side of this issue, Baumrind believes she can disprove Kohlberg's theory by citing a single negaitve case. But this obviously cannot succeed unless the individual clearly satisfies all the appropriate conditions. In fact, a single negative case seldom falsifies any complex scientific theory, since it can always be questioned whether the exception really satisfies the necessary conditions (Brandt, 1959, p. 242). In the case of moral development, numerous extraneous factors (see section V) could prevent a particular individual from applying formal operations to moral issues in the manner specified by the theory.

II

Baumrind implies that R. S. Peters and W. P. Alston share her doubts about the universality of Kohlberg's developmental sequence as well as the metaethical justification of stage 6 principles. In fact, neither writer seriously criticizes Kohlberg on these points, despite their other doubts and questions. Peters challenges neither the empirical evidence for a universal sequence of cognitive justice-structures nor the metaethical argument that rational men would, under appropriate conditions, acknowledge the two stage 6 principles. His point is rather that there are other moral motivations and character traits that also call for developmental analysis. As Peters (1971) states his thesis, "I have certain doubts . . . (which) derive from the thought that there is much more to morality than is covered by his theory, and that his generalizations may be true only of the area of morality on which he has concentrated his attention" [p. 238]. Peters specifically, and I believe rightly, challenges Kohlberg to further clarify the logical bases of moral development, the role of moral instruction, and the relationship of character traits and motives to cognitive principles in moralization. His principal point is that there are motivational dimensions of morality that supplement Kohlberg's study. But Peters nowhere questions the possibility of an invariant sequence of justice-structures culminating in universalizable substantive rules.

In contrast with Peters, Alston does question three of the metaethical (as distinguished from empirical) criteria for establishing the superiority of stage 6—namely, differentiation, integration, and prescriptivity. But he nowhere questions the possibility of justifying the ethical principles recognized at stage 6. In fact, Alston (1971) calls for a more finely articulated metaethical defense of stage 6 as "a morally superior way of resolving moral problems" [p. 277]. Hence, Baumrind cannot legitimately enlist Peters and Alston in support of her "negative case" against stage 6 principles. What is needed to support this case is a thoroughgoing critical analysis of the evidence for the theory and the metaethical arguments undergirding the substantive rules involved, but this is precisely what Baumrind fails to provide.

III

Baumrind accuses me of a subjectivism similar to her own, because I also employ the first person singular. There is a crucial difference, however, between my statement, "I believe psychologists are *rationally compelled* (insofar as they assume a moral perspective) . . ." and her frequent justification of moral claims by statements like "As an atheist I reject," "I view the Good Life as . . . ," "My definiiton of course is personal," and so forth. My statement explicitly indicates that publicly persuasive reasons justify my position. By contrast, many of her statements do justify normative claims on purely subjective grounds. Baumrind's explicit rejection of emotivism in her second paper does not repudiate subjective appeals; it rather confirms my initial suggestion that she does not really intend to rest the entire case for rule-utilitarianism on exclusively subjective motivations.

Yet, Baumrind again reverts to pure subjectivism in her admittedly irrational defense of her personal system of values in the conclusion of "It Neither Is Nor Ought To Be." Despite irresoluable conflicts with her own utilitarian calculations vis-à-vis the common good, Baumrind argues that other values are "justified by a personal system" of some sort. But this simple detour around the metaethical question is obviously unsatisfactory, since almost anything could be justified on these grounds. Moreover, Baumrind' acknowledged inconsistency in rejecting her own utilitarian criterion in the name of unspecified personal values suggests that she does not really have an ethical position at all, but rather a variety of competing and inconsistent values to which she appeals for reasons that escape comprehension, not to mention justification.

IV

Baumrind charges Kohlberg and myself with relying on intuitionism to justify the superiority of stage 6 principles, despite our explicit rejection of precisely this type of metaethical theory. Her reasoning, as far as I can determine, is that nonutilitarians necessarily depend upon self-evident propositions or special insights. If intuitionism refers to the metaethical thesis that normative principles are justified by direct apprehension of nonnatural moral qualities, it is clearly incompatible with fundamental presuppositions of developmental psychology in the Piagetian tradition. For Piagetians reject innate ideas and special insights into an alleged nonnatural realm of values for a perspective that views morality as a self-constructive process involving organism-environment interaction. Kohlberg's (1971) rejection of intuitionism is crystal clear:

> the existence of six qualitatively different systems of moral apprehension and judgment arising in invariant order is clear evidence that moral principles are not the intuitions of an inborn conscience or faculty of reason of the sort conceived by Butler or Kant. And if stages of moral judgment develop through conflict and reorganization, this is incompatible with the notion that moral judgment is a direct apprehension of ... non-natural facts [p. 184].

Elsewhere, I have argued that intuitionism is unacceptable as a metaethical theory, because it fails to provide an adequate basis for distinguishing veridical from false intuitions (Wallwork, 1972, p. 191).

V

Baumrind's argument that highly sophisticated thinkers, like Nietzsche and Ayn Rand, have not defended stage 6 reasoning misconstrues moral development as an exclusively cognitive process.

Intellectual sophistication involving formal operations is a necessary, but not a sufficient, condition for the attainment of the higher stages of moral reasoning. The sufficient condition is the central capacity for role-taking which distinguishes social cognition from cognition of physical objects. Essentially, role-taking involves the ability "to react to others as like the self, and to react to the self's behavior from the other's point of view" [Kohlberg, 1971, p. 190]. This capacity, which begins in infancy, gives rise to successive justice structures as the growing individual attempts to balance the competing claims of men: "you versus me; you versus a third person" [Kohlberg, 1971, p. 192]. Just as Piaget's interpretation of logic moves toward an equilibrium of cognitive operations, Kohlberg interprets morality as moving toward an equilibrium integrating discrepant moral claims by means of "reversibility," a process which assures that everyone receives equal treatment in similar circumstances.

Highly sophisticated thinkers might well fail to develop the highest levels of moral reasoning due to inadequate environmental opportunities for role-taking, failure to develop sympathetic role-taking abilities, and/or deficient application of cognitive operations to specifically moral issues. In other words, one might be cognitively sophisticated, but deficient—as "character disorders" vividly illustrate—in areas crucial for moral development. Moreover, a person may understand stage 6 principles but desire not to apply them for a variety of emotional or egoistic reasons. As Kohlberg (1971) observes:

> One reason for the assymetry between cognitive level and level of moral judgment might be that cognitive potential is not actualized in moral judgment because of a will, or desire, factor. It is obviously to one's self-interest to reason at one's highest level in the cognitive realm, less clearly so in the moral realm. Stage 6 may be the cognitively most advanced morality, but perhaps those *capable* of reasoning that way do not wish to be martyrs like Socrates, Lincoln, or King, and *prefer* to reason at a lower level [p. 188].

A more likely source of this failure in application than fear of martyrdom is the desire of privileged individuals to protect economic and social benefits. But the essential point is that a variety of factors account for divergent ethical opinions among sophisticated men and women. Far more important than the mere existence of diverse moral judgments among intelligent people, which Baumrind emphasizes, is whether persuasive reasons for alternative principles are presented, and this is precisely what she fails to demonstrate.

VI

Baumrind rightly inquires regarding the "logic" that compels "morally sensitive" individuals to embrace stage 6 principles of justice. But she incorrectly attributes to me the doctrine of "ethical logicalism" which holds that the validity of ethical statements can be established on exclusively logical grounds. If this were my position, I would have argued that the capacity to reason logically is sufficient to establish the truth of fundamental ethical norms. In addition to the obvious inconsistency of this exclusively logical view with the importance of role-taking in the Kohlbergian scheme, I explicitly emphasized "moral sensitivity" in my remarks to draw attention to the fact that valid ethical reasoning presupposes being capable of assuming the so-called moral point of view. As defined by the long tradition of impartial observer theorists from Hume and Adam Smith through Baier (1958), Firth (1952), and Frankena (1963), the distinctively moral perspective or attitude that assures correctness in decision-making involves impartiality, consistency, generalizability, conceptual clarity, and full information about all relevant facts. Metaethically, judgments or principles are justified if they hold up under sustained scrutiny involving these criteria that define the moral point of view (Frankena, 1963, p. 95).

Although a full defense of these criteria of the distinctively moral perspective is beyond the scope of this paper, a crucial argument in their favor is the fact that we normally employ them both to discount and to confirm ordinary moral judgments. For example, we discount a moral opinion by saying: "He was biased or insufficiently impartial." "He inconsistently applies to minority groups (women, blacks, research subjects, and so on) a treatment of which he would complain if applied to himself." "He would not have done that if he had not been fatigued, ill, or confused." "The case should be retried, because the court did not have all the facts about the case." Similarly, we strive for correct moral decisions in public institutions—like the courts, investigating commissions, and the like—by assuring, as far as possible, impartiality, consistency, generalizability, conceptual clarity, and full knowledge of all relevant facts. When these conditions are not met, we are inclined to doubt or to question the rightness of the resulting decisions. My point here is that these everyday criteria constitute a metaethically valid decision-making procedure for establishing the rightness and wrongness, goodness and badness of acts and rules.

Incidentally, Kohlberg errs in neglecting to specify these criteria of the moral point of view, presumably because he falsely believes that they result in stage 5 moral conclusions. However, the foregoing criteria are fully compatible with his interpretation of the "impartiality" involved in reversible role-taking as well as with the criteria of universalizable consistency, generalizability, and comprehensive integration of factual information that characterize stage 6. It is because these specific criteria are realized by stage 6 moral reasoning that it is superior to the other stages, not because it is the last on a developmental hierarchy involving "differentiation," "integration," and "prescriptiveness." The latter criteria, Alston rightly argues, have to do with mere logical sequence and do not metaethically justify the superiority of the final stage. But Alston fails to discuss the metaethical criteria of "the moral point of view" that *do* validate stage 6 principles.

Among several crucial "reasons" for moving to stage 6 principles are the serious limitations of the rule-utilitarianism of stage 5, at least when evaluated in terms of considered judgments based on the distinctively moral point of view. One of the most serious defects of rule-utilitarianism is the failure of "the greatest possible net good" criterion to equitably distribute the rights, privileges, burdens, and duties of social life. For example, suppose we have to choose between two rules—rule A and rule B—with almost, but not quite, identical consequences. Rule A has *slightly* better consequences, but it also distributes the goods or privileges of society to a relatively small group of people, while rule B spreads slightly fewer goods and privileges equally among a large portion of the population. The rule-utilitarian would be forced to conclude that rule A is superior to rule B, but this violates our considered judgment that a slightly greater gain for the few does not compensate for the losses to the many. This problem of unequal distribution is even clearer if we consider another set of rules ($R1$ and $R2$) with identical consequences. When the benefits realized by the rules are equal, Frankena (1963) observes,

In Defense of Substantive Rights

> the rule-utilitarian may say that $R1$ and $R2$ will serve equally well as principles of right and wrong and that there is no basis for choosing between them. But it still may be that they distribute the amount of good realized in different ways: acting on $R1$ may give all the good to a relatively small group of people without any merit on their part (to let merit count at this point is already to give up utilitarianism), while acting on $R2$ may spread the good more equally over a large part of the population. In this case . . ., we must and would say that $R1$ is an unjust rule and that $R2$ is morally preferable [p. 33].

In other words, rule-utilitarianism appproves of *any* rule for distributing privileges and burdens that maximizes the balance of good over evil, but the resulting calculations often violate considered judgments about equitable distribution. The principles of utility and justice are thus distinct, and the latter is capable of overriding the maximization proposal.

Faced with these objections, rule-utilitarians often modify their proposals to enjoin "the greatest good of *the greatest number*." But then, as Frankena (1963) points out, they are really recommending two principles, since we are enjoined "(1) to produce the greatest possible balance of good over evil and (2) to distribute this as widely as possible" [p. 34]. In other words, this proposal really abandons pure utilitarianism for a mixed position recognizing a principle of justice alongside utility. But, then, the principle of justice requires separate articulation and defense. Baumrind's ethical theory will remain implausible until she demonstrates a convincing way of handling these standard problems with all forms of utilitarianism.

In addition to the equitable distribution problem, *some* rule-utilitarian proposals—and here I would definitely include those of the APA and Baumrind—are so imprecise about intrinsic goods as to permit widespread violation of generally recognized human rights. Essential to all rule-utilitarians are more or less clear assumptions regarding the intrinsic good(s) to be realized by rules, although proponents differ markedly according to whether the good is defined as pleasure, happiness, liberty, knowledge, or a plurality of these and/or other values. The APA code apparently considers liberty (or self-determination) as an intrinsic good, inasmuch as the rules weigh against deceit and promote informed consent. But the code is sufficiently vague about other intrinsic values which cannot be secured by following the rules (e.g., knowledge, alleviation of human ills, and so on) as to permit easy disregard of the code in the name of act-utilitarian appeals to these other values.

Baumrind arrives at more stringent rules by stressing the intrinsic good of self-determination, but her other criteria are no less imprecise and dangerous to generally recognized rights. On utilitarian grounds, Baumrind readily sacrifices the rights of various categories of people in order to realize alleged benefits for the majority. In this spirit, she recommends not only punishment of, but even "revenge" against, evil doers with no mention of the rights that individuals possess independently of the consequences of their behavior. The right of informed consent is denied by Baumrind to "the insane, the convicted criminal, and the dependent minor" without regard for their other rights, because "society" allegedly does not consider them fully responsible. Distributive justice is viewed solely in terms of merit, although even utilitarian calculations on the basis of declining marginal utility of income would suggest at least a minimum standard of living apart from meritorious accomplishments (Brandt, 1959, chap. 16). Finally, and most seriously, all individual rights are subordinated by Baumrind to the larger, but undefined, "good" of the community:

> In accordance with rule-utilitarianism, an act is judged right if and only if the rule under which it falls will probably produce a balance of good over evil for man as a species. Where the good of the species and the good of the subgroup do not conflict, then the act should also maximize the good of the subgroup. Where the good of the species and the subgroup do not conflict with the good of the individual, then the act should maximize the good of the individual as well.

Without a clear specification of what "good" means in this context, such a proposal could have odious consequences, especially given the propensity of nation-states to identify parochial interests with those of humanity. But this serves to illustrate another problem—beyond ambiguities about intrinsic goods—with the Baumrind and APA formulations. Like stage 5 subjects, they tend to treat human life in terms of its instrumental contribution to community welfare rather than in terms of universal respect and acknowledgment of rights that exist prior to the person doing anything.

There are, to be sure, more sophisticated rule-utilitarian theories that succeed in avoiding both ambiguities about intrinsic goods as well as instrumental valuations of human life. Some express stage 6 principles by incorporating concepts of justice within utilitarian schemes, although these concepts are not finally justifiable on utilitarian grounds. But I am primarily concerned here with Baumrind's request for "reasons" for transcending stage 5 moral arguments. Stage 5 includes such undesirable components as an instrumental valuation of human life, a tendency to allow formally proper procedural processes (like obtaining consent from research subjects) to take priority over protection of ongoing rights, and a tendency to limit justice to "liberty," typically defined as freedom of contractual consent and equality of opportunity.

Baumrind believes I am guilty of circularity in arguing against these and other stage 5 propositions because I seem to assume the validity of the alternative norms that I propose to justify. The appearance of circularity is probably impossible to avoid in any complicated ethical discussion. But no circularity is involved in my argument as a whole, since I assume that the moral point of view specifies the criteria for correct moral decision making in all circumstances. The question is whether these criteria really do justify the twin principles of equal regard and equal weighing of claims. It is to this issue that I would now like to turn.

As John Rawls persuasively argues in *A Theory of Justice*, the criteria of impartiality, consistency, generalizability, and relevant information can be brought into operation by imagining an original contractual situation in which men are to set up the social rules by which they will be governed when society comes into being. Impartiality is assured by a "veil of ignorance" which makes it possible for the contractors to have all relevant knowledge of social life except the positions they will occupy and the natural talents they will possess in the future social order. Deprived of this biasing information, they are to determine the principles that will govern the distribution of social rights and duties, benefits and burdens, powers and immunities. The resulting principles of justice, Rawls (1971) argues, will be general in form, universal in application, and publically recognized as the "final court of appeal for ordering the conflicting claims of moral persons" [p. 135]. Under these ideal decision-making conditions, "rational men"—who are minimally defined by Rawls as concerned with maximizing their individual self-interests—would not agree to a utilitarian principle maximizing the algebraic sum of advantages, precisely because they might suffer from the resulting distribution. Instead, they would protect themselves in all social positions by choosing to be governed by two substantive principles of justice. The first requires the greatest equal liberty compatible with a like liberty for all. The second (the difference principle) permits only those inequalities in the distribution of primary social and economic advantages that benefit everyone.

The first principle defines and secures "political liberty (the right to vote and to be eligible for public office) together with freedom of speech and assembly; liberty of conscience and freedom of thought; freedom of the person along with the right to hold (personal) property; and freedom from arbitrary arrest and seizure as defined by the concept of the rule of law" [Rawls, 1971, p. 61]. This first principle is prior in the sense that these basic liberties cannot be sacrificed in the name of social and economic advantages, unless the latter are sufficiently scarce so as to preclude meaningful exercise of basic liberties. The Rawlsian rationale is thus more egalitarian about liberty than about other goods, such as wealth, power, and prestige; the ordering does not permit exchanges of basic liberties for economic and social gains.

The second principle insists that inequalities in wealth, authority, power, and other social advantages benefit all groups. Any departure from equality of social benefits must be acceptable to everyone in the sense that all would prefer the life prospects with the inequalities to those without them. This distributive principle does not mean that every single individual must benefit from a social inequality; rather, it insists that each social stratum must benefit from the inequality in ways that result in each stratum being better off than it would be without the inequality. This precludes utilitarian calculations supporting differences in the distribution of social benefits on the grounds that the disadvantages to one group are outweighed by the greater advantages to others. The inequalities must benefit all strata, a stipulation which places the burden of proof on those claiming privileges. The latter must demonstrate how privileges in wealth, authority, or power will benefit all social strata, especially the worst off.

This Rawlsian rationale is especially important for our purposes, because it employs the criteria of the moral point of view so as to justify and to further clarify stage 6 principles. The first stage 6 principle that "persons are of unconditional value" means that each person is valued qua human existent, not because he is such-and-such a person with idiosyncratic qualities and accomplishments. A fundamental equality exists which prevents one person from being valued less highly than another. This is spelled out by Rawls in terms of equal respect for the basic liberties of all men: freedom of conscience and thought, political rights, and freedom from arbitrary treatment. These clarifications of the "equal regard" principle are sufficient to counter Baumrind's charge that all such appeals are vacuous.

The second stage 6 principle, "the right of every person to an equal consideration of his claims in every situation," is protected by the priority of the equal liberty criterion. This precludes the possibility of ever disregarding basic liberties with an eye to social benefits, e.g., the use of research results. The second stage 6 principle also is protected by the distributive criterion that everyone benefit from inequalities in the allocation of income, authority, power, and offices.

The above specification of stage 6 principles supported several of my specific recommendations at the Loyola symposium. With respect to equal liberty, I suggested that researchers could not legitimately violate the basic liberties of subjects. The freedom to do research, I stated, is limited by the rights of subjects; and those who transgress these rights of equal liberty cannot consistently claim similar rights. Given the priority of equal liberty, I argued that cost-benefit calculations are unacceptable because they override basic liberties in the name of potential benefits. Where less than full information is provided consenting subjects, I suggested, the researcher must demonstrate that the withheld information does not infringe on the basic liberties protected by the informed-consent criterion. With regard to the distributive principle, I also argued that deprivations to research subjects could only be justified if it was clear that everyone would agree, if they fully identified with all parties, that the benefits sufficiently outweighed the deprivations as to lead everyone, if fully informed of all relevant aspects of the situation, to agree to the study. Because the poor and minority groups are already unjustly treated in American society, I argued that "deprived groups have a special claim not to have additional burdens in the form of research studies placed upon them."

VII

Baumrind claims that my definition of rule-utilitarianism as a procedural process conflicts with Kohlberg's observation that this rationale can support the substantive principles contained in the Bill of

Rights. She further contends that the two substantive principles regarding equal respect and just treatment are merely tacked onto these rights, although they are no more rationally persuasive than those derived from the rule-utilitarian criterion. No conflict is involved, however, since I presupposed Kohlberg's discussion of stage 5 and merely emphasized his point that the rationale for rights at this stage rests on a procedural process designed to transcend relativism through group consensus. However, I did add the observation that the use of rule-utilitarian procedures by various professional groups could result in diverse rules respecting the rights of subjects. This is a likely consequence because not all rule-utilitarian proposals emphasize identical intrinsic goods and some, like the new APA code, are considerably less stringent than were the framers of the Bill of Rights regarding the protection of basic liberties.

The only utilitarian means of rectifying the moral dilemma resulting from diverse calculations is to stress, as Baumrind does, the priority of the intrinsic good of liberty (or self-determination), and to construct stringent rules regarding informed consent, deceit, honesty, and so forth, to assure realization of this good. Even those who take this position, however, are apt to adopt a means-end schema which occasionally violates substantive rights in the name of other values (as previously observed regarding Baumrind's theory) or to assume that formal consent legitimates otherwise unethical behavior. The latter occurs when researchers misrepresent genuine risks in order to obtain consent and use the formal consent to violate substantive rights.

More importantly, even a carefully constructed rule-utilitarian theory centering on liberty is unable to handle the issue of unjust distribution. Consequently, additional injustices may be heaped upon deprived groups for the benefit of the privileged.

VIII

Baumrind finds my use of "universal" equivocal, because she fails to attend to the important distinction, which I presuppose, between universal and universalizable. The term "universal" refers to the factual possibility of resolving moral disputes. Cultural relativists deny the possibility of moral agreement by contending the "fundamental" disagreements regarding moral principles preclude any form of rational resolution. This *factual* issue is obviously quite different from the metaethical task of justifying ethical principles by specifying the criteria for establishing the truth of ethical claims. Yet, this factual issue regarding whether or not moral disagreements are "fundamental" and irreconcilable does effect the metaethical enterprise. For cultural relativism often is used to support the skeptical metaethical claim that no method of reasoning can demonstrate that one ethical position is right and another wrong. Kohlberg's research is important because it counters widespread assumptions regarding fundamental cross-cultural moral disagreements and the impossibility of resolving disputes involving justice. His work could be disproved, however, and Duncker's (1939) famous critique of cultural relativism would still stand—namely, the virtual impossibility of proving the existence of irreconcilable moral disagreements. Baumrind has not responded to the latter argument against moral relativism in my first paper.

The term "universalizable" refers to one of the conditions for justifying normative claims. The universalizable criterion is thus very different from the factual question regarding whether or not universal agreement is possible. The usual argument in favor of this criterion is that moral judgments logically commit one to making similar judgments about similar cases. What is right for one person must be right for every other person in a relevantly similar circumstance. What you claim for yourself, every man has the right to claim for himself unless you can give persuasive reasons that explain why the principle applies in the one case and not in the other.

The confusion Baumrind experienced in interpreting my remarks apparently derives from the fact that Kohlberg's "universal" sequence of justice-structures culminates in a mode of reasoning that employs the "universalizable" criterion along with the other criteria of the distinctively moral point of view. Whether or not Kohlberg's universal stage theory is correct, his stage 6 principles are metaethically justified because they are universalizable, impartial, and so forth.

IX

Baumrind objects to my "final stage" characterization of stage 6, but there is nothing in my paper that implies a terminal point in the advancement of moral reasoning. Kohlberg's "bare bones" sketch of stage 6 principles obviously requires further specification, and Rawls (1971) readily admits that his procedural rational needs to be applied to other ethical principles besides justice (pp. 108–117). Personally, I see no reason why human thought about ethical issues should not progress, as it has progressed in the past, by means of criticism, reformulation, and so forth.

Baumrind's comments about "postmoral" or postrational" stages of existence introduce extraneous considerations irrelevant to the philosophical justification of principles of justice. Because these transcendent "stages" have to do with faith in a world-view involving deep emotional motivations, they deal with the question: "Why be moral?" But this issue is quite different from the one under discussion, namely: "How do we justify ethical principles?" The relationship between these very different questions will be thoroughly discussed by Kohlberg, Fowler, and myself in our forthcoming book on deveolpmental theories of religion.

X

Baumrind's contention that I am guilty of employing stage 3 and 4 moral arguments (in appealing to recent developments in contemporary philosophy and the federal courts) misconstrues the point of these comments. Public discussions of this sort are relevant not because they issue from authorities, but because they tend, through mutual criticism, to correct distortions of the moral perspective, namely, biases, self-interests, inconsistencies, conceptual confusions, incorrect information, and so forth. A single individual may be biased, insufficiently informed of relevant facts, and the like, but these failures tend to be corrected by sustained public debate. To be sure, politically motivated judicial appointments work against realization of these criteria in the courts, but I believe judicial decisions no less than philosophical essays contain important arguments for and against seemingly viable ethical options that deserve careful consideration on the part of those claiming ethical competence. Baumrind apparently disagrees, but her own failure to consider commonly recognized objections to her ethical theories indicates the importance of attending to public discussions of this sort.

XI

Baumrind detects an inconsistency in my appeal to consequences as well as to substantive principles only because she incorrectly supposes that deontological theories necessarily preclude consequential analysis. I know of no contemporary deontological theory, however, that ignores consequences. The Rawlsian rationale which I employ actually requires consequential analysis in assessing the results of different social arrangements of rights, privileges, and powers. What deontologists reject is the utilitarian assumption that all ethical decisions can be forced into an exclusively consequential mode of analysis.

Baumrind correctly objects, however, to the ambiguity of my statement about the possibility of benefits sufficiently outweighing violations of rights so as to permit some studies involving less than fully informed consent. I did not mean to imply, as she supposes, that benefits justify fundamental violations of basic liberties. This is why I prefaced the remarks she cites with a clause (which she fails to cite) about full identification with, or consideration of, the prior rights and interests of subjects. On these grounds, less than fully informed consent in research involving some forms of deceit may be permissible, if subjects are not exposed to risks and the benefits are significant. Where risks are involved, however, I do not see how researchers can justify exposing subjects without their full knowledge and truly voluntary consent.

XII

Baumrind is unquestionably correct that my recommendations regarding surrogate group discussions and review committees do not prevent these groups from reaching decisions that violate substantive rights. No procedural process in human affairs ever precludes unethical or illegal results. I certainly did not imply, as Baumrind suggests, that *any* committee decision is ethically justified. The point of these recommendations is to "lean against" the biases, self-interests, and other factors that result in unethical decision-making on the part of researchers.

XIII

Baumrind views my policy recommendation to the *American Psychologist* as a form of coercion reminiscent of stage 2 subjects (although she probably means to refer to stages 1 or 3). The point of my recommendation is not punishment, however, but the protection of unsuspecting human being from unscrupulous treatment. Baumrind apparently believes consistent application of stage 6 principles would result in the abolition of legal and other regulatory procedures. On the contrary, man's proclivity for harming others by violating substantive rights will always necessitate the institutionalization of rules and laws back by sanctions. The latter are justifiable by forms of moral-reasoning principles of justice superior to the primitive punishment orientations found at stages 1 and 3.

XIV

Baumrind believes that stage formulations necessarily lead to an "intolerant and parochial denigation of so-called lower-level thinking." But she fails to note that genuine regard for every other human being includes a fundamental respect for the moral and intellectual views of others which precludes precisely this sort of denigration. If any position threatens to denigrate others, instrumental valuations in terms of accomplishments (Baumrind's "merit") would appear to do so.

Baumrind's negative characterization of stage theories is especially curious given her use of an unspecified stage theory to support the superiority of rule- over act-utilitarianism in her first paper. In any case, the ethical position that I have been defending does not depend upon, though it is supported by, stage formulations. It rests, instead, on a metaethical decision-making procedure which is independent of stage sequences. If Kohlberg is right, however, one would have to attain formal operations to comprehend the form of reasoning involved.

XV

I am baffled by Baumrind's reference to Wozniak's (1973) paper in criticizing Piaget and myself for being insufficiently aware of dialectical logic, since Wozniak's thesis is that Piaget *is* a dialectical theorist. Kohlberg's theory is similarly dialectical in its application of Piaget's research to moral reasoning. Apparently, Baumrind's point is that a seemingly noncontradictory position at stage 6 may contain contradictions which will eventually necessitate new dialectical reconstructions. If this is her position, I agree with her. I certainly agree with her trivial point that a formally correct syllogism is unacceptable if it is based on faulty premises or relationships. But I require reasons for rejecting plausible premises beyond her simple emotivist assertions in the form: "I simply reject *p*." I would think Baumrind's own objections to intuitionism would invalidate her claim that "unless the conclusion 'proven' by the relation between the premises is acknowledged as true even without justification, the justification offered will not prove persuasive."

In discussing logic, Baumrind accuses me of being insufficiently dialectical in the statement: "Baumrind seems driven by the logic of her second line of reasoning to the unsatisfactory emotivist position that ethical claims are merely reflections of subjective desires...." Yet, the point of this sentence is precisely that she attempts to combine two very different lines of thought. The real thrust of Baumrind's criticism here is not that I fail to recognize both sides of her argument, but that I refuse to accept those arguments in her paper that are based on purely subjective grounds. Her real complaint is not that I am unaware of dialectical logic, but that I refuse to join her particular form of the dialectical argument. I refuse to do so precisely because this side of her argument fails to provide sufficient reasons for anyone else accepting her subjective decisions. I am leary of subjective arguments in ethics, because anything can be justified on these grounds.

XVI

Baumrind contends that the *data* do not support my statement that "Kohlberg's research explicitly demonstrates that the disagreements she (Baumrind) cites between philosophers, like Kant and Mill, are theoretically resolvable at the highest stage of moral reasoning." There are really two points here. The first has to do with whether or not Kohlberg's research supports a universal and invariant sequence of justice structures. The second has to do with whether or not the metaethical criteria that are built into Kohlberg's characterization of stage 6 indicate that these disputes are "theoretically resolvable." Taking the second, and philosophically more important, issue first, the ethics of both Kant and Mill are obviously inadequate when surveyed from the moral point of view. This is why no one today accepts their arguments in the form in which they left them. Yet, the problems with these theories are resolvable along stage 6 or Rawlsian lines.

With regard to the empirical foundations of universal justice structures, the situation is more complex. The unpublished papers by Simpson (1973), Holstein (1973), and Kurtines and Greif (1973) raise critical issues that deserve careful consideration and additional research. But the several criticisms gleaned by Baumrind from these sources are scarcely as destructive as she supposes.

Baumrind's first criticism is that Kohlberg's own research undermines the universal hypothesis, because (1) postconventional reasoning was not discovered among subjects in the two primitive villages in the Yucatan and Turkey, (2) stage 3 predominated among urban boys in Taiwan and Mexico, and (3) stage 5 predominated only among urban middle-class boys in the United States. But these findings are precisely what the theory predicts. In primitive societies where alternative norms and values are generally unknown, the necessary conditions for transcending conventional morality are absent. Moral development is slower among urban adolescents in Taiwan and Mexico than in the United States for perfectly understandable factors having to do with awareness of nonconventional moral options and opportunities for critical reflection. The major research finding, which Baumrind ignores, is that stages 5 and 6 *were* found among subjects in both Taiwan and Mexico. These results suggest that postconventional reasoning is not an exclusively culture-bound phenomena.

Second, Baumrind asserts that Kohlberg's new scoring manual invalidates his earlier cross-cultural studies. Apparently, she is unfamiliar with the relevant changes. None substantially alter the gross scores. Most of the changes deal with refinements and with the scoring of transitional subjects between conventional and postconventional stages (the result being the new stage 4½).

Third, Baumrind asserts that Holstein's unpublished study empirically invalidates Kohlberg's assumptions regarding invariance and irreversibility. However, there are a number of problems with the Holstein study, especially the use of self-administered tests and the scoring of transitional subjects. Generally, Holstein's research confirms Kohlberg's work. The principal negative finding indicates the possibility of regression, but the results may be the product of incorrect scoring. By way of contrast, all of Kohlberg's longitudinal studies confirm the invariant and irreversible nature of moral development. Baumrind's uncritical acceptance of Holstein's research contrasts sharply with her tendency to reject Kohlberg's own research findings.

Finally, Baumrind offers several irrelevant criticisms of her own. For example, she claims that Buddhists, Christians, Marxists, and others differ regarding the "good life." But Kohlberg's research deals with "justice," not concepts of the "good." The latter are notoriously variable, but they are separable from the principles of justice involved in the treatment of research subjects. Because justice, not the good, is the principal issue at stake in the debate over the APA code, Baumrind merely diverts attention from this focus with her frequent references to personal values or the good life.

Incidentally, Baumrind also claims that Kohlberg's stories are unreal, because they minimize emotional involvement. But this bracketing of emotions is obviously necessary in order to study cognition. Because emotional involvement is minimized, Baumrind does not believe responses to Kohlberg's dilemmas predict actual behavior. But she completely ignores the evidence of a positive correlation between moral cognition and behavior. In any case, the issue separating the APA, Baumrind, and myself concerns valid ethical decision making, not emotional behavior.

XVII

Baumrind concludes her essay with several absurd charges regarding my alleged Gnosticism and intolerance. Since the charge of Gnosticism rests upon the unfounded assertion that I claim special insight or knowledge (as contrasted with Baumrind's other charge that I rest ethics solely on empirical data), it is sufficient to observe that rational arguments, not intuition, provide the basis for my position in ethics. As for my alleged intolerance, I neither denigrate others nor fail to appreciate that "truth is a human product brought into being by the interaction among individuals." I disagree with the APA code and with Baumrind's ethical theory (insofar as she has one) for publically recognizable reasons, but these do not lead me to depreciate anyone. For understandable reasons, Baumrind's charges strike me as expressing precisely the derogatory attitude attributed to me, since I stand accused of being an intolerant Gnostic. More importantly, however, intolerance and disparagement can be found among representatives of all ethical positions, including dogmatic relativists and emotivists. Fortunately, the validity of an ethical position does not rest with these variable character traits, but with the plausibility of the reasons that support it.

BIBLIOGRAPHY

Alston, W. P. Comments on Kohlberg's "From is to ought." In T. Mischel (Ed.) *Cognitive development and epistemology.* New York: Academic, 1971.
Baier, K. *The moral point of view.* Ithaca, N. Y.: Cornell University Press, 1958.
Brandt, R. B. *Ethical theory.* Englewood Cliffs, N. J.: Prentice-Hall, 1959.
Brandt, R. B. *Value and obligation: Systematic readings in ethics.* New York: Harcourt, Brace and World, 1961.
Brandt, R. B. (Ed.) *Social justice.* Englewood Cliffs, N. J.: Prentice-Hall, 1962.
Dunker, K. Ethical relativity. *Mind,* 1939, **48**, 39–57.
Firth, R. Ethical absolutism and the ideal observer. *Philosophy and Phenomenological Research,* 1952, **12**, 317–345.
Frankena, W. K. *Ethics.* Englewood Cliffs, N.J.: Prentice-Hall, 1963.
Frankena, W. K. The ethics of love conceived as an ethics of virtue. *The Journal of Religious Ethics,* 1973, **1**, 21–36.
Freund, P. Legal framework for human experimentation. *Daedalus,* 1959, 314–324.
Hannaford, R. V. "You ought to derive 'ought' from 'is.'" *Ethics,* 1972, **82**, 155–162.
Hare, R. M. *Freedom and Reason.* London and N. Y.: Oxford University Press, 1963.
Hare, R. M. "Rawls' theory of justice." *The Philosophical Quarterly,* 1973, **23**, 144–155, 241–252.
Holstein, C. B. Moral judgment change in early adolescence and middle age: A longitudinal study. Paper presented at the biennial meeting of the Society for Research in Child Development, Philadelphia, March 29–April 1, 1973.

Katz, J. *Exprimentation with human beings.* New York: Russel Sage Foundation, 1972.
Kohlberg, L. The development of modes of moral thinking and choice in the years ten to sixteen. Unpublished doctoral dissertation, University of Chicago, 1958.
Kohlberg, L. Moral development and identification." In H. Stevenson (Ed.) *Child psychology, 62nd Yearbook of the National Society for the Study of Education.* Chicago: University of Chicago Press, 1963.
Kohlberg, L. Cognitive stages and preschool education. *Human Development,* 1966, 9, 5–17.
Kohlberg, L. Early education: A cognitive-developmental approach. *Child Development,* 1968, 39, 1013–1062.
Kohlberg, L. The child as a moral philosopher. *Psychology Today,* 1968, 2, 25–30.
Kohlberg, L. Stage and sequence: The cognitive-developmental approach to socialization. In D. Goslin (Ed.) *Handbook of Socialization Theory and Research.* New York: Rand McNally, 1969.
Kohlberg, L. Stages of moral developmnet as a basis for moral education. In C. Beck & E. Sullivan (Eds.) *Moral education.* Toronto: University of Toronto Press, 1970.
Kohlberg, L. Education for justice: A modern statement of the platonic view. In T. Sizer (Ed.) *Moral Education.* Cambridge, Massachusetts: Harvard University Press, 1970.
Kohlberg, L. From is to ought: How to commit the naturalistic fallacy and get away with it in the study of moral development. In T. Mischel (Ed.) *Cognitive development and epistemology.* New York: Academic Press, 1971.
Kupperman, J. J. The supra-moral in religious ethics: The case of Buddhism. *The Journal of Religious Ethics,* 1973, 1, 65–72.
Kurtines, W., & Greif, E. B. The development of moral thought: A review and evaluation of Kohlberg's approach. Unpublished paper, 1973.
Lyons, D. *Forms and limits of utilitarianism.* Oxford: Clarendon Press, 1965.
Olafson, F. A. *Justice and social policy.* Englewood Cliffs, N. J.: Prentice-Hall, 1961.
Peters, R. S. Moral developments: A plea for pluralism. In T. Mischel (Ed.), *Cognitive development and epistemology.* New York: Academic, 1971.
Rawls, John. Justice as fairness. *Philosophical Review,* 1958, 68, 164–194.
Rawls, J. *A theory of justice.* Cambridge, Mass.: Harvard University Press, 1971.
Simpson, E. L. Moral development research: A case study of scientific cultural bias. Unpublished paper, 1973.
Wallwork, E. *Durkheim: Morality and milieu.* Cambridge, Mass.: Harvard University Press, 1972.
Wozniak, R. H. Structuralism, dialectical materialism, and cognitive developmental theory: An examination of certain basic assumptions of Piagetian theory. Paper presented at the biennial meeting of the Society for Research in Child Dvelopment, Philadelphia, March 1973.

APPENDIX

Excerpts from "Ethical Principles in the Conduct of Research with Human Participants"

American Psychological Association

THE ETHICAL PRINCIPLES

The decision to undertake research should rest upon a considered judgment by the individual psychologist about how best to contribute to psychological science and to human welfare. The responsible psychologist weighs alternative directions in which personal energies and resources might be invested. Having made the decision to conduct research, psychologists must carry out their investigations with respect for the people who participate and with concern for their dignity and welfare. The Principles that follow make explicit the investigator's ethical

Source: Ad hoc Committee on Ethical Standards in Psychological Research, "Ethical Principles in the Conduct of Research with Human Participants" (Washington, D.C.: American Psychological Association, 1973), pp. 1–2, 18–19, 21–22, 27–28, 29, 39–42, 52–54, 58–59, 61, 75–77, 81–83, 87–89. Copyright © 1973 by the American Psychological Association, Inc. Reprinted by permission of the publisher.

responsibilities toward participants over the course of research, from the initial decision to pursue a study to the steps necessary to protect the confidentiality of research data. These Principles should be interpreted in terms of the context provided in the complete document offered as a supplement to these Principles.

1. In planning a study the investigator has the personal responsibility to make a careful evaluation of its ethical acceptability, taking into account these Principles for research with human beings. To the extent that this appraisal, weighing scientific and humane values, suggests a deviation from any Principle, the investigator incurs an increasingly serious obligation to seek ethical advice and to observe more stringent safeguards to protect the rights of the human research participant.

2. Responsibility for the establishment and maintenance of acceptable ethical practice in research always remains with the individual investigator. The investigator is also responsible for the ethical treatment of research participants by collaborators, assistants, students, and employees, all of whom, however, incur parallel obligations.

3. Ethical practice requires the investigator to inform the participant of all features of the research that reasonably might be expected to influence willingness to participate and to explain all other aspects of the research about which the participant requires. Failure to make full disclosure gives added emphasis to the investigator's responsibility to protect the welfare and dignity of the research participant.

4. Openness and honesty are essential characteristics of the relationship between investigator and research participant. When the methodological requirements of a study necessitate concealment or deception, the investigator is required to ensure the participant's understanding of the reasons for this action and to restore the quality of the relationship with the investigator.

5. Ethical research practice requires the investigator to respect the individual's freedom to decline to participate in research or to discontinue participation at any time. The obligation to protect this freedom requires special vigilance when the investigator is in a position of power over the participant. The decision to limit this freedom increases the investigator's responsibility to protect the participant's dignity and welfare.

6. Ethically acceptable research begins with the establishment of a clear and fair agreement between the investigator and the research participant that clarifies the responsibilities of each. The investigator has the obligation to honor all promises and commitments included in that agreement.

7. The ethical investigator protects participants from physical and mental discomfort, harm, and danger. If the risk of such consequences exists, the investigator is required to inform the participant of that fact, secure consent before proceeding, and take all possible measures to minimize distress. A research procedure may not be used if it is likely to cause serious and lasting harm to participants.

8. After the data are collected, ethical practice requires the investi-

gator to provide the participant with a full clarification of the nature of the study and to remove any misconceptions that may have arisen. Where scientific or humane values justify delaying or withholding information, the investigator acquires a special responsibility to assure that there are no damaging consequences for the participant.

9. Where research procedures may result in undesirable consequences for the participant, the investigator has the responsibility to detect and remove or correct these consequences, including, where relevant, long-term aftereffects.

10. Information obtained about the research participants during the course of an investigation is confidential. When the possibility exists that others may obtain access to such information, ethical research practice requires that this possibility, together with the plans for protecting confidentiality, be explained to the participants as a part of the procedure for obtaining informed consent.

* * *

III. COMMENTARY ON THE ETHICAL PRINCIPLES

Section 1-2. The Decision For or Against Conducting a Given Research Investigation

The basic problem faced by the investigator in planning research is how to design the study so as to maximize its theoretical and practical value while minimizing the costs and potential risks to the humans who participate in it. A particular study is ethically unacceptable to the extent that its theoretical or practical values are too limited to justify the impositions it makes on the participants or that scientifically acceptable alternative procedures have not been carefully considered.

There are a number of long-established and reasonably effective mechanisms for assuring the soundness of the psychologist's judgment concerning the best ways to maximize the basic and applied scientific values of his research. Graduate training programs in psychology, critical reviews of research reports by editorial consultants for journals and books, and evaluations of research proposals by panels of experts who advise funding agencies all help to educate the researcher in assessing whether the results of an investigation will have scientific or practical value—though the investigator should be aware that his personal investment in his own research ideas may lead him to exaggerate the potential contribution of his proposed study.

Less well developed, however, are professional mechanisms for assuring that the costs and risks to the human participants are accurately assessed and kept to a minimum. While the mechanisms for assessing scientific value are not indifferent to the costs of research to the participants, they have been more conspicuously concerned with assessing the scientific quality of the research. Only in recent years (and often only in response to student complaints or specific directives from federal agencies) have we seen the wide-spread establishment of a formal mechanism —the department "subject pool" committee or the institutional ethics review committee—dedicated primarily to safeguarding the welfare of human participants in research. Every study makes some impositions on the participants that, while typically quite minimal may sometimes be appreciable. It is probably often the case that they are assessed as less serious by the investigator than by the participant or an outside observer.

The investigator, therefore, must ascertain whether it would be ethically responsible to conduct the research he has in mind when one takes participants' costs as well as scientific and social gains into account. Are the risks and costs to the participants so serious as to rule out the study, or to require its radical redesign, no matter how great its potential value? Or, does the research promise to contribute so much to psychological science or to society or even to the welfare of the participants themselves that it should be carried out even though it imposes great demands on them? Answering these questions involves facing complex issues. If the research is done, might it harm the participant or contribute to a social climate of manipulation, suspicion, and lack of trust? Is the development of a science of human behavior and experience so vital to the survival of our complex society that to fail to conduct the research is to abdicate one's basic obligation as a psychological scientist? Is the psychologist ever justified—and perhaps even obligated—to conduct research that exposes human participants to severe physical or mental stress?

These and many other questions must be considered by the investigator in the initial, fundamental decision to conduct, to modify, or even to abandon the research he has in mind. What are the possible gains from the research that its abandonment will forego, and what kind of impositions on the participants or on society might be made by carrying it out? How can the researcher check his own subjective and biased judgments in reaching a decision? When and where and on what issues should the researcher obtain advice in difficult situations? In collaborative research, where does the responsibility reside for making the decision to proceed or to abandon the research?

* * *

Principles

Many of the research descriptions submitted by APA members bore on the researcher's decision for or against conducting a particular investigation on the basis of his weighing the scientific and social gains from proposed research against the anticipated impositions on the research participants. Some psychologists are inclined at least on first consideration of the problem, to offer a simple absolute rule that one may never do research if it imposes some loss upon the participants. But further examination of the issue leads most people to a more complex judgment that there are matters of degree and circumstances that must be taken into consideration. Most human experiences and social interactions impose losses as well as gains upon the individuals involved, and research does not differ in this respect. Moreover, the decision not to act is itself an ethical choice that can be as morally reprehensible as deciding to act.

One must look more closely into the specifics of the situation and its complexities in drawing up ethical guidelines. One has to take into account the degrees of loss and gain and their likelihood. But such accounting involves extremely subjective judgments that are vulnerable to systematic biases. In order to reach a fair judgment in such cases, therefore, it is essential to employ certain procedural safeguards such as securing prior advice from sensitive consultants and obtaining the free and informed consent of the participant. But the researcher cannot abdicate or dilute his own final responsibility.

Principle 1. In planning a study the investigator has the personal responsibility to make a careful evaluation of its ethical acceptability, taking into account these Principles for research with human beings. To the extent that this appraisal, weighing scientific and humane values, suggests a deviation from any Principle, the investigator incurs an increasingly serious obligation to seek ethical advice and to observe more stringent safeguards to protect the rights of the human research participant.

The further question of locus of responsibility for deciding whether to undertake or abandon the research arises when several investigators are involved in the conduct of research (as co-investigator, or as senior investigator and assistant, or as teacher and student). Such collaborative situations multiply rather than divide the responsibility, so that each of the parties bears full responsibility. For example, both the principal investigator who designed the research and the assistant who conducts it are fully responsible for safeguarding the welfare of the participants.

Principle 2. Responsibility for the establishment and maintenance of acceptable ethical practice in research always remains with the individual investigator. The investigator is also responsible for the ethical treatment of research participants by collaborators, assistants, students, and employees, all of whom, however, incur parallel obligations.

* * *

Section 3-4. Obtaining Informed Consent to Participate (Including Issues of Concealment and Deception)

The psychologist's ethical obligation to involve people as research participants only if they give their informed consent rests on well-established traditions of research ethics and on strong rational grounds. The individual's human right of free choice requires that the decision to participate be made in the light of adequate and accurate information. The fairness of the implied agreement between investigator and the research participant (Section 6, pp. 52–58) also rests upon the latter's informed consent.

Ethical problems arise because the requirements of effective psychological research often conflict with the simple fulfillment of this obligation to obtain informed consent. The relevant information may be too technical for the person to evaluate. In most tests of quantitative hypotheses, for example, the theory is beyond the research participant's comprehension. In the field of psychophysiology, the processes being studied may be completely unfamiliar to the participant. In many cases, the degree of discomfort or embarrassment to be experienced that would be relevant to the decision to participate may not be fully ascertainable prior to the conduct of the research. Certain classes of people (e.g., children, the mentally retarded, psychotics) may be incapable of responsible decision. By far the most common reason for limiting information, however, is that if the individual were to be fully informed about the purpose and procedures of the research and of the experiences to be anticipated, valid data could not be obtained. Methodological requirements of the research may demand that the participants remain unaware of the fact that they are being studied or of the hypotheses under investigation. Incomplete information or misinformation may have to be provided to elicit the behavior of a naive individual, or to create a psychological reality under conditions that permit valid inference.

These research requirements present the investigator with frequent ethical dilemmas. Under what circumstances, if any, is it acceptable to bypass, delay, or compromise acting on the obligation to give the person full information about the research and obtaining on this basis the required consent or refusal to participate? About what aspects of the research must information be provided? The issues that are involved here are closely entwined with ones subsequently examined in Section 5, Assuring Freedom from Coercion to Participate. They also touch upon considerations relating to the responsibility of the investigator to provide clarifying information at the end of a study (Section 8-9, pp. 75–87). This section provides a discussion of issues that center on the *informed* component of "informed consent"; the *consent* component appears in Section 5. Since deception, when it is employed in research, intrinsically compromises the information upon which consent is gained, it is considered here. It is to be noted, however, that, in addition, deception involves bad faith and thus raises a second and more serious ethical concern. For this reason, a separate principle is devoted to deception (Principle 4) rather than treating it entirely within the context of informed consent.

* * *

Principles

From the introductory statement of the problem, and from the incidents just presented, it is clear that the ethical ideal of obtaining fully informed consent cannot be realized in much research without a serious risk that the results of the research will be deceptive or misleading. In addition, technical aspects of the research may exceed the limits of what participants can comprehend. Principles 3 and 4 are statements that may provide helpful guidelines to ethical behavior for the investigator who must cope with the complex problems of informed consent and deception.

Principle 3. **Ethical practice requires the investigator to inform the participant of all features of the research that reasonably might be expected to influence willingness to participate, and to explain all other aspects of the research about which the participant inquiries. Failure to make full disclosure gives added emphasis to the investigator's responsibility to protect the welfare and dignity of the research participant.**

Principle 4. **Openness and honesty are essential characteristics of the relationship between investigator and research participant. When the methodological requirements of a study necessitate concealment or deception, the investigator is required to ensure the participant's understanding of the reasons for this action and to restore the quality of the relationship with the investigator.**

* * *

Section 5. Assuring Freedom from Coercion to Participate

This section deals with the extent to which it is ethically acceptable to bring pressure to bear upon people to participate in psychological research. The issue is complex and involves matters of philosophical importance. Complete freedom of choice is a cherished human ideal and coercion of any sort is an abridgment of that freedom. At the same time it must be recognized that hundreds of years of philosophical analysis of the problem under rubrics such as "free will" and "determinism" have neither completely clarified these concepts nor provided us with the necessary rules of ethical conduct. What does it mean to speak of the research participant's "freedom of choice" when one considers that such choices are the lawful psychological consequences of past and present influences in the environment? And how can we propose that a person deciding whether or not to participate in research should be free from coercion and at the same time maintain that all decisions are motivated and that they are affected by forces that act upon the decision maker?

Obviously the empirical materials that lie behind the discussion in these pages will not answer questions at such a basic philosophical level. What they can do, however, is to show two things: (*a*) that the problem of coercion in research with human beings arises in connection with a particular kind of influence—that which characterized situations where a person in a position of power uses that power to force another person to participate in research, and (b) that the exercise of such coercion varies a great deal in the extent to which it seems to exploit the research participant. Depending upon the circumstances, these instances range all the way from simple askings of favors to coercive demands that any observer would agree are unacceptable whatever his position on the more basic philosophical question.

The use of coercive measures to obtain the cooperation of participants in research is widespread. "Subject pools" consisting of all of the students enrolled in certain psychology courses exist in many universities. Employees in business and industry are required to participate in research under conditions where they might perceive refusal as placing their jobs in jeopardy. The participation of military personnel may be required under circumstances that virtually rule out resistance.

In instances that occupy extreme positions on a dimension of coerciveness, most observers would probably agree that the procedures used to secure consent to participate in research either are or are not ethically objectionable. For example, most people would probably agree that it would be unethical for an investigator doing research in a prison setting to force prisoners to submit to a highly dangerous research manipulation on the threat that failing to comply would put the prisoner's chance of being paroled in jeopardy. By contrast, almost no one would regard it as unethical to induce a college student to take part in a typical memory experiment by offering him payment for an hour's participation.

The worrisome examples fall between these extremes. To illustrate, even so conventional an incentive as money may become unduly coercive. A person in dire financial need, for example, the prisoner without money to buy cigarettes, might agree to participate in a hazardous experiment for a very small sum whereas others would ask a thousand times as much. In this case, is the exploitation of the prisoner's special situation not unethical? On the other hand, would it not be even more unethical to diminish the prisoner's freedom by withholding the opportunity? To consider another example, how coercive is it to threaten a patient with the denial of therapy for refusing to take part in an experimental study of the effectiveness of the therapeutic agent? Denial of a desperately needed service is generally seen as reprehensible but is there not something particularly appropriate in the case of the patient that warrants making research participation a condition of obtaining such a service?

So far we have mentioned only a few of the inducements that are used to motivate research participation. The range of such inducements is, of course, quite wide. Besides financial and other material rewards, moral appeals are used, such as promising the individual the satisfaction of knowing he has contributed to the advancement of science or to the solution of social problems, or that he has helped the researcher or some highly valued reference group. Or appeals are made on the basis of friendship, the positive value of cooperation, or the special needs of the investigator. Can this moral suasion ever become unduly coercive? To what extent is it permissible to use social pressure or statements that refusal to participate is a sign of uncooperativeness, lack of courage, and the like?

The problem of coercion sometimes arises even with persons who initially had no objection to taking part in the research. Having agreed to participate they may find the procedures painful, threatening, or more boring or time consuming than anticipated. Presumably freedom from undue pressure to participate should not end at the start of the experiment. Does a research participant surrender freedom of choice after deciding to participate or does such freedom continue to exist in the form of the option to drop out of the research at any point? Is the researcher ever permitted to impose a penalty for dropping out? If the person does not complete his participation, may the investigator withhold all or part of the promised payment? How far is the researcher obliged to go in repeatedly bringing the opportunity to drop out to the participant's attention? To what extent and by what means might it be permissible to urge a reluctant participant to continue because, for example, allowing participants to drop out may bias the data?

* * *

Principle

Freedom of choice is a human value in its own right. It is particularly important in research because of its relationship to other ethical problems discussed elsewhere in this document. The need for freedom from coercion becomes increasingly pronounced to the extent that research participation entails risks or costs of any type to the participant. The following principle attempts to capture this ideal and, at the same time, to recognize the complexities that are discussed further in sections to follow.

Principle 5. Ethical research practice requires the investigator to respect the individual's freedom to decline to participate in research or to discontinue participation at any time. The obligation to protect this freedom requires special vigilance when the investigator is in a position of power over the participant. The decision to limit this freedom increases the investigator's responsibility to protect the participant's dignity and welfare.

* * *

Section 6. Fairness and Freedom from Exploitation in the Research Relationship

The relationship between the investigator and the research participant is one of mutual respect and involves considerations of fairness or equity. Each party to the relationship has expectations of the other, which in the ideal case will be accurate and congruent with one another. The agreement to take part in an experiment usually implies that the participant is willing to provide research data at some personal cost of time and effort and perhaps unpleasantness or risk in order to receive, in return, certain benefits. The expected benefits may be tangible rewards in the form of money or goods; they may be personal help such as counseling or therapy; they may be informational as, for example, a satisfactory explanation of the purposes of the experiment and its relationship to the current state of knowledge in some field. They also may be the satisfaction of feeling one has advanced science, helped solve a social problem, or done a favor for the researcher. Ethical problems arise when too much is asked of the participant given the anticipated benefits, when the investigator fails to keep his part of the bargain, and when he exploits the participant's personal circumstances in order to obtain cooperation.

The agreement between the investigator and the research participant can be evaluated from a dual perspective: (*a*) The agreement itself should be fair in the judgment of the participant. (*b*) The investigator should keep whatever promises he makes. Ideally there should be a reciprocal provision of benefits and good faith on the part of the participant, too, but we are concerned here only with the obligations of the investigator.

The researcher's obligation to the research participant are not easy to establish with clarity, for several reasons: (*a*) The expected and actual benefits to the participants are difficult to assess; (*b*) some potential participants—for example, mental patients, children, and the mentally defective—may not be able to understand the proposed agreement; (*c*) in other cases, the personal situation of the individual may influence what seems fair. A person feeling great need of some service such as psychotherapy would be willing to take greater risks and to sustain greater costs to obtain this help than would a person without such a felt need; (*d*) finally, some of the investigator's obligations exist only by reasons of the implications of the research setting. Such intangibles are, of course, particularly difficult to assess.

How explicit does the agreement between investigator and participant need to be? How can the investigator tread the thin line between offering adequate inducements to participate and exploitation (which amounts also to coercion to participate: See Principle 5)? When the possibility of exploitation is manifest, how may the responsible investigator nevertheless safeguard the interests of the participant?

* * *

Principle

The ethical investigator must be concerned with the fairness of whatever implicit or explicit agreements are made with the participants. He incurs the responsibility to assure that the participants' reasonable expectations are realized. In appraising the fairness of the agreement, the investigator must guard against exploiting the special needs and vulnerabilities of the potential participants to gain their cooperation. The guiding principle can be stated thus:

Principle 6. Ethically acceptable research begins with the establish-

ment of a clear and fair agreement between the investigator and the research participant that clarifies the responsibilities of each. The investigator has the obligation to honor all promises and commitments included in that agreement.

* * *

Section 7. Protection from Physical and Mental Stress

In most psychological research, the participants are exposed neither to appreciable physical suffering or danger nor to appreciable mental stress. The relatively rare studies involving physical stress or danger are typically undertaken to clarify important topics such as motivation or the nature of pain and its relief. The investigator may be studying the stressful state itself (e.g., the effects of drugs on pain suppression), or he may use deprivation, electric shock, or intense noise to manipulate motivational or incentive conditions.

Mental stress also is absent from most psychological research, but in some studies it may arise as an essential aspect, in others, incidentally, and in still others, accidentally. It may be the essential independent variable, as when the researcher exposes participants to varying levels of failure in order to study the effects of loss of self-esteem on ways of coping or to temptations to lie or cheat in order to study moral functioning and development. In other studies, the mental stress involves a less essential aspect of the research, as when different levels of anxiety are induced in order to study the effects of drive level on stimulus generalization. In still other cases, the mental stress involves a less essential aspect of the research, as when different levels of anxiety are induced in order to study the effects of drive level on stimulus generalization. In still other cases, the mental stress arises accidentally, as when some participants are embarrassed by certain questionnaire items in ways difficult to anticipate or when the participant unexpectedly develops feelings of having done poorly on a learning task.

Responsible investigators obviously would not expose research participants to actual or potential physical or mental harm if there were not a very serious reason for doing so. Although some psychologists feel that such research should be entirely prohibited, the dominant view in the field is probably that when such studies are important they should be continued. Under what circumstances is research involving physical or mental stress or danger permissible?

Studies that raise this question are relatively rare partly because investigators are ingenious enough to find alternate ways of studying the research problem at issue. For example, much research on deprivation employs non-human animals, or uses deprivations or stresses that are relatively trivial in type and amount, or studies persons who are under going differential amounts of deprivation or mental stress for reasons independent of the research and beyond the investigator's control.

Where such alternatives cannot be found, might the importance of the research counterbalance the appreciable costs to the participant? When the investigator decides that research involving physical or mental stress is warranted, what measures should be taken to protect the welfare of the participants?

* * *

Principle

The researcher may find himself in conflict between the obligation to carry out research which he feels might yield important human benefits and the obligation to avoid treating participants in that research in ways that are likely to expose them to appreciable levels of physical or mental stress. In resolving these conflicting obligations, the researcher must weigh the amount and probability of the stress which he is likely to produce and the number of participants who might experience it against the possible benefits that the research might yield. Research that involves physical or mental stress or risk of harm may be conducted only for highly important purposes and only after a thorough search for alternatives to minimize danger or discomfort. A decision that such a study is ethically warranted requires that safeguards to protect the participant be commensurate with the stress or risk that is involved. Such a decision may be reached responsibly only after full technical and ethical consultation. Principle 7 summarizes the investigator's responsibilities. It implies that the principles relating to informed consent to participate (Principle 3), to fairness and freedom from exploitation in the research relationship (Principle 6), and to removal of stressful consequences following completion of the research (Principle 9) must be scrupulously observed—with compromise in these principles not to be tolerated insofar as the stress or risk is serious.

Principle 7. The ethical investigator protects participants from physical and mental discomfort, harm and danger. If the risk of such consequences exists, the investigator is required to inform the participant of that fact, secure consent before proceeding, and take all possible measures to minimize distress. A research procedure may not be used if it is likely to cause serious and lasting harm to participants.

* * *

Section 8-9. Responsibilities to Research Participants Following Completion of the Research

The investigator has the obligation to assure that research participants do not leave the research experiencing undesirable aftereffects attributable to their participation. Such negative consequences can arise if the participants are permitted to remain confused or misinformed about important aspects of the study or, more serious still, if steps are not taken to remove effects of psychological stress or other painful consequences resulting from research participation.

Section. 8: Clarifying the Nature of the Research to the Participant at the End of the Study

Committing human resources to psychological research is justified by the need to advance knowledge about human experience and behavior. The research psychologist has a primary obligation to conduct such research with procedures most likely to advance knowledge and increase understanding. As discussed above in Section 3-4, however, many investigators assert that the best research procedures sometimes necessitate giving participants certain misconceptions about themselves or about events occurring during the study. In other cases such misconceptions, though not deliberately induced by the investigator, occur during the course of the study.

The responsible investigator feels an obligation not only to remove any misconceptions which the participant develops during the research but also to provide a full appreciation of facets of the study not revealed during participation. These may include the full particulars about the problem under investigation, the broader significance of the research, how the research might contribute to the solution of the problem, and the value of the role played by the participant in this process.

In Section 3-4 above, we have considered in detail the various circumstances which may justify the investigator in sometimes inducing or permitting the occurrence of certain misconceptions during the course of an investigation. Whenever conditions such as these prevail, the investigator is faced with a number of difficult questions. For example, is he always obligated to correct misconceptions, even if he did not instill them deliberately? Is the investigator always obligated to check for misconceptions, even when none were deliberately induced? Must the lack of information or the misconceptions be corrected immediately or may the correction wait until all participants have completed the experiment—or until any given participant has completed all the sessions? Must the investigator correct misinformation or provide missing information even when this will be distressing to the participant? What modifications of usual procedures are required when the research participants are children? These and related questions identify the central concern of this section.

* * *

Principle

The need to conduct research in a way that makes it maximally informative and minimally misleading may cause the investigator to withhold from the participant certain information or even to misinform the participant during the time when data are being actively collected. Once this participation is completed, however, reasons for allowing the participant to be misinformed or uninformed generally no longer obtain, and the investigator is obliged to provide full clarification. This is especially important where continuation in the misinformed or uninformed state might have some deleterious effect on the participant. There are various reasons why immediate clarification is important. The longer that the uninformed or misinformed state persists, the greater the likelihood that it will be integrated into the participant's though system, and lead to other errors or to inappropriate action. Also, the longer it persists, the more likely it is that the subsequent disclosure will have a detrimental impact on the participant's feeling of trust in interpersonal relationships. Practically, too, it becomes increasingly difficult to locate the participant and to motivate attendance at a session in which clarification may be presented.

Principle 8. After the data are collected, ethical practice requires the investigator to provide the participant with a full clarification of the nature of the study and to remove any misconceptions that may have arisen. Where scientific or humane values justify delaying or withholding information, the investigator acquires a special responsibility to assure that there are no damaging consequences for the participants.

* * *

Sec. 9: Removal of Stress and Other Undesirable Consequences of Research Participation

A great deal of psychological research causes no appreciable stress or other major costs to the human participants. The experienced investigator, however, soon becomes aware that occasionally even the most innocuous research can inadvertently give rise to stress and leave the participant feeling anxious or inadequate. Simple cognitive tasks involving short-term memory or decision making can leave the individual worried about possibly performing quite poorly; or filling out harmless personality inventories may induce in the participant worries about whether he has some unsuspected pathological symptoms. Similarly, painless physiological recording devices may result in the participant's feeling frightened and perhaps worried that he lacks courage. Children, owing to their more limited range of experience, are particularly likely to misunderstand research procedures or to misinterpret, in highly surprising ways, routines and procedures that seem quite unthreatening to the investigator.

The humane researcher designs the study so as to minimize the likelihood of such undesirable side effects. Even after taking appropriate precautions, it is necessary to remain sensitive to the vulnerability of people to draw disturbing inferences from the atypical situations in which they are placed during psychological research. This requires careful checking for possible detrimental effects after the study is over and being prepared to apply appropriate means to remove such effects when they are found.

In other research, stress of a psychological or physical nature occurs not by inadvertence, but as an intrinsic and deliberately planned part of the investigation. Included here are studies involving the effects of pain or failure which were discussed in Section 7 on protection from physical and mental stress. Assuming that such studies are done, the ethical investigator is careful to remove any detrimental effects they produce as soon as the study is completed.

Finally, there are a number of related problems, such as withholding beneficial treatment from control subjects and whether, when possibly damaging information about the participant emerges during the research, this ought to be withheld from the person.

* * *

Principle

Sometimes intentionally and sometimes unintentionally, an investigator may use research procedures that produce negative aftereffects in the research participants. Given that this will happen, it is necessary that researchers become alert to such developments. Once they are detected, it is obligatory that efforts be made to remove them.

Principle 9. Where research procedures may result in undesirable consequences for the participant, the investigator has the responsibility to detect and remove or correct these consequences, including, where relevant, long-term aftereffects.

* * *

Section 10. Anonymity of the Individual and the Confidentiality of Data

The ethical obligations related to maintaining anonymity and confidentiality derive from a widely accepted rule of human conduct. This rule is that every person has a right to privacy as regards most aspects of life which only that person can give permission to violate. Various threats to this right of privacy sometimes occur in research with human beings. On the one hand, the investigator may obtain private information about people without their knowledge. This raises ethical issues related to informed consent treated in Section 3-4 of this report. But, in addition, the investigator, having obtained information about research participants, with their informed consent, may pass it on to others later. In so doing, an expectation of confidentiality may have been violated. Problems of this type are the subject of discussion in this section.

The central issue has many facets. For one thing, it is clear that maintaining confidentiality is more important for certain types of information than others. Religious preferences, sexual practices, income, racial prejudices, and other personal attributes such as intelligence, honesty, and courage are more sensitive items than "name, rank, and serial number." However, there are undoubtedly great individual differences in the resistance different people would offer to the disclosure of different types of personal information. This consideration argues for a conservative stance, according to which the investigator should be very cautious about revealing any information about research participants.

Another aspect of the problem involves the recipient of the information that is divulged. It is no doubt one thing to reveal to a participant's physician evidence of possible drug usage by the person but quite another to provide the local police with the same information. Either disclosure entails serious ethical considerations, but the potential threat to the individual is almost certainly greater in the latter case than in the former.

Requests for confidential information may come from many sources— the research participant's relatives and friends, officers of the law, employers, school administrators, the custodians of data banks, even the investigator's professional associates. The demands can be so varied that no simple list can be exhaustive. Again it seems clear that the investigator must take a position that will protect the research participant from many threats to confidentiality, some of them unexpected.

In some cases the problem may arise in ways that involve valued groups rather than the research participant as an individual. Many people, by choice, might regard it as a breach of confidence for an investigator to publish information they disclosed which would tend to degrade their sex, racial group, hometown, or social fraternity. Such considerations mean that the issue of confidentiality can even come up in connection with the publication of research results without specific identification of the participants.

Finally, some particularly difficult problems arise when the investigator, often by accident, obtains information that perhaps *should* be disclosed either for the research participant's own protection or the protection of others. It is not uncommon for an investigator to learn that the research participant uses hard drugs, has suicidal thoughts, desperately fears failure in college, habitually carries a gun, or is trying to lose weight on a diet that is known to be dangerous to his health. What are the ethical responsibilities of the investigator who discovers information such as this?

* * *

Principle

These incidents demonstrate that issues of anonymity and confidentiality are not as clear-cut as they are sometimes thought to be. To the contrary, there are plausible claims from many directions for information the researcher may acquire about research participants. Sometimes the act of protecting their identity and holding facts about them in confidence seems to conflict with the rights, rather than simply the desire, of others to know. In extreme cases, maintaining confidentiality may prevent actions needed to protect the welfare—and even the lives—of the participants themselves.

Despite these complications it seems clear that the investigator's primary responsibility is to fulfill the expectation of anonymity and confidentiality with which the research participant enters the research relationship. Principle 10 reflects this position.

Principle 10. **Information obtained about the research participants during the course of an investigation is confidential.** When the possibility exists that others may obtain access to such information, ethical research practice requires that this possibility, together with the plans for protecting confidentiality, be explained to the participants as a part of the procedure for obtaining informed consent.

Index

Alston, W. P., 85, 105, 106, 110
American Psychological Association, 34, 77, 90, 111, 112
APA Code of Ethics, 2, 4, 6, 48–50, 53, 59, 64, 65, 70, 72, 73, 75, 76, 79, 91, 100, 101, 111, 112, 116, 123, 124
Aristotle, 42, 45, 91, 92

Baumrind, D., 2, 7, 70, 71, 85, 92, 95, 101, 103–124
Bill of Rights, 44, 87, 115, 116

Christianity. *See* Judaeo-Christian Morality
Cook Committee Report. *See* APA Code of Ethics
Cost Benefit Analysis, 10, 49–51, 59, 73, 76, 89–91, 115
Culture, 38, 71, 96
 acculturation, 26
 cultural relativism, 96, 116, 122, 123
 technological culture, 30

Deception. *See* Research
Deontology, 41, 42, 83–91, 101, 104, 119
Developing Nations, 17, 18

Ecology, 17
 bioethics, 27
Emotivism, 92–93, 106, 121, 124
Ethical Principles in the Conduct of Research with Human Participants. See APA Code of Ethics

Fletcher, J., 43, 49
Frankena, W. K., 109, 110, 111
Freud, S., 47
Futurology, 14, 15
 utopias, 20

Gnosticism, 100, 123, 124

Humanistic Psychology, 7, 16

Informed Consent. *See* Research
Intuitionism, 41, 85, 95, 100, 104, 107, 121

Judaeo-Christian Morality, 27–29, 31, 38, 40, 96, 123
Justice, 45, 74, 75, 104, 105, 113, 114, 118, 120, 122, 123
 commutative justice, 45
 distributive justice, 46, 75, 112, 115
 retributive justice, 45

Kant, I., 40–42, 46, 70, 95, 96, 101, 107, 122
Kierkegaard, S., 89, 101
Kohlberg, L., 39, 71, 73–75, 85–89, 92, 94–97, 104, 105, 107–110, 115–118, 120–123

McCormick, R. A., 68
Manipulation. *See* Research
Marxism, 21, 41, 86, 96, 123
Mead, M., 78
Milgram, S., 60–61
Mill, J. S., 40, 41, 55, 70, 95, 122
Miranda v. *Arizona*, 76
Moore, G. E., 41
Moral Reasoning, 83–98, 104, 105, 108, 109, 110
 moral convictions, origin of, 24–25, 46
 the moral point of view, 109–110
 reversibility, principle of, 75, 108
 role taking, 78, 108, 109
 universalizability, principle of, 79, 80, 88, 94, 95, 96, 97, 110, 117
 universal principles, 86, 87–88, 90, 95, 96, 116
Nationalism, 112
Nietzsche, F., 45, 55, 86, 107

Old Age, 30

Peters R. S., 85, 105, 106

Piaget, J., 88, 91, 104, 107, 108, 121
Platt, J., 14, 21
Population, 17, 18

Race Relations, 12
Rand, A., 86, 107
Rawls, J., 113–115, 118, 119, 122
Research, 63, 75, 77, 98, 115, 119
 deception and manipulation, 48, 55, 59, 61–63, 65, 78, 79, 90, 111, 116, 119
 with human subjects, 8, 62, 66
 informed consent, 34, 51, 52, 54, 63, 76, 77, 79, 111, 112, 116, 119
 social contact 55–56, 74
Rieff, P., 26
Role Taking. *See* Moral Reasoning

Situation Ethics, 41, 43, 49
Skinner, B. F., 7, 13, 14, 15, 16, 20
Smith, M. B., 70, 101, 102
Social Contract. *See* Research

Teaching, 13
Teleology, 41, 43, 84, 101
 act teleology, 63
 rule teleology, 43, 51, 63
Testing, 12, 97
 I.Q. tests, 12, 18
Therapy, 9
 group therapy, 9
 human services, 9, 10, 11
Thielicke, H., 29

Utilitarianism, 74, 106, 107, 112, 113, 119
 act utilitarianism, 43, 44, 50, 51, 52, 72, 112, 120
 rule utilitarianism, 43, 51, 55, 71, 72, 86, 87, 90, 96, 101, 106, 110, 111, 112, 115, 116, 120
Utopias. *See* Futurology

Wallwork, E., 83, 102
Wozniak, R. H., 91, 121

Zen Buddism, 39, 40, 84, 86, 89, 96, 123